PLAY THROUGH THE FOUL

THE FOUL

Basketball Lessons for the Game of Life

To Michele ~
Vera Jones 2015

VERA JONES

PUBLISHED BY VOICEWORKS MEDIA
10920 Baymeadows Road, #27-140
Jacksonville, Florida 32256
www.VerasVoiceWorks.com

ISBN: 978-0-9840929-0-1

DEDICATION

In memory of my mother, Mary K. Jones.
You are my constant inspiration. Your love, laughter and
support live on in me, encouraging me to inspire others.
I miss you terribly, but thank God it's not too
late to listen to my mother.

ACKNOWLEDGMENTS

To my "3-D family": Drew, Dad and DJ, I love you always. To Aunt Delcie who I love and deeply miss. To Jan Bethea for being my most unconditionally loving, loyal and supportive friend and business partner. To Stephen Soleyn for making friendship, laughter and family work despite our fouls. To GMA's Robin Roberts for believing in me and for being a consummate model of strength, courage and professionalism. To Mo Davenport for giving me my first "big chance," and to Brian Sherriffe and Dick Vitale for your honest and kind words of encouragement at ESPN. To agents Wendi Huntley and Kris Kellam-Jernstedt for your guidance and friendship. To AJ Ali and Karen Hunter who were my strongest influencers to honor God and to write. To Mona-Gail Baker who convinced me Play Through the Foul was an awesome concept and title. To my editor Dawn Josephson for your literary wisdom and guidance. To Summer Morris, David Wanika and Joe Anzalone for great work and guidance with design, printing and photography, respectively. To Pila Gray who worked a financial miracle for me I will never forget. To my Syracuse Orangwomen team mates and alumni for being winners both on and off the court. To Carmen Bland, Ted Davis, Jr., Cherie Hogg, Monica Maxwell, Denise Saul, Tamika Simmons, Stephanie Wilkins, Teresa Waters, John Willis, Jr., and countless family members, friends, student athletes and business associates who believed in me, this project and this book.

Most especially to God... Thank you for life here humbly and complete with fouls, and for Christ's gift of eternal life gloriously free from them.

CONTENTS

PRE-GAME....

I was five years old when I first fell in love....with a basketball. I know you may be wondering what a five-year-old girl could possibly know about love, but I was an early bloomer. When I was three I had a bit of a crush on Ernie and Bert from Sesame Street. But it wasn't until the day I held a basketball in my hands that I really began to experience this special and personal connection that lasted for the rest of my life.

I fell fast and hard into this love affair, one whose years of union would outlast my favorite pets, my closest friends and even my marriage. I didn't know it then, but undeniably I had met my soul mate. The lessons I would come to learn from playing, coaching and commentating on the game of basketball ultimately shaped my life, offering me creative perspectives on such things as setting goals, celebrating triumphs and overcoming adversity. It's what eventually brought me to write this book.

Play Through the Foul™ is a collection of true stories from my life, although I've withheld or changed some of the names to protect those who might suffer a coronary to find parts of their lives revealed in print. This book is my personal account of how the game of life is very much like the game of basketball. We are all trying to take our best shot to win, but we often get fouled or suffer defeat along the way.

Eight of my most memorable, personal life stories of tragedy, transition or triviality are revealed in the **Off the Court** segment of each chapter. The basketball lessons or anecdotes follow in the **On the Court** segment. Thus, the direct or indirect pain and tragedy of experiences such as abuse, divorce, death of a loved one, loss of a job or homelessness that I've experienced off the court, I matured through with an on the court basketball perspective.

The Game Plan

This is not a strategic or technical "basketball book" strictly for sports enthusiasts. The principles revealed within these pages, such as getting yourself into shape, making the assist, handling pressure, rebounding, being mentally tough and focusing on the goal, are lessons intended for anyone who has ever suffered a foul while playing this contact sport called "life."

We know that playing any contact sport often involves the risk of personal injury. But we play anyway for the thrill, exhilaration, adventure and the intimate gratification we want to achieve on so many levels by doing so.

Additionally, you don't need to be a basketball guru to know what a foul is. On the most simplistic level, we all know that fouls hinder and hurt. I wrote this book to share with you how I've played through some of my life's fouls in hopes that I might encourage you to passionately and strategically play through your own.

Play Through the Foul™ is intended to inspire and empower you to realize we are all being constantly conditioned, tested and seasoned for growth, maturity and purpose. We are all incessantly aiming for the goal we've set for ourselves (or others have set for us) to win. Quite honestly, playing the game isn't always easy, and it's not always fun. However, even when we are convinced we are ready to give up, give in or get away, what we still desire most is to win. While we each may define winning according to our individual desires, our greatest triumphs in life are those which have been orchestrated by God, our "Ultimate Coach" and Creator. Peace, love and joy are those simplistic victories we're all playing for.

There's a champion that lives within all of us. How we choose to play the game determines whether that champion comes out to claim his or her true crown.

Ready, Set, Shoot

It has been said that any sport is a microcosm of society, and that we all are truly players in the game of life. I believe this to be true in so many ways and have celebrated many of life's victories as well as suffered my share of defeats. I've cried a little, but laughed a lot! And I wanted to write a book that would elicit a response in readers to do the same.

Over the years I've come to realize that sometimes it's the little things that seem to foul us the hardest. And there's nothing like a good laugh at ourselves or our crazy predicaments to make our loads seem a little lighter. That's why I've chosen to share not just the painful experiences, but also the seemingly silly ones, like my ridiculous workout regiments to demonstrate the power of focusing on the goal to get in shape, or a battle with a cockroach to illustrate the importance of standing up for yourself and defending your territory. It's all still part of the game.

The comparisons and parallels of sports, particularly basketball, to this game we call life are astounding. How do I know? Because my friends and broadcast audiences tell me I use them (sometimes ad nauseam) all the time!

This book is dedicated to so many of those people who have said, "Vera, you crack me up with your basketball analogies. You should write a book." It is dedicated to the friends, family and student-athletes I have shared "one-on-one" time with who have told me I've offered them wise and helpful advice in a creative or humorous way. A decade or so later, here I am folks!

I wanted to have written this book sooner, but I got hammered driving through the lane a few times, turned the ball over a few more, and just flat out didn't bring my A-game along the way. So thanks for waiting!

Score this book as a personal victory because it satisfies my desire to make yet another "assist," which has gradually become a character and lifestyle choice for me. Early in my career, I was the "shooter," the "gunner," the "star." And quite honestly, for a little while, that's all I really cared about. Over time I've learned the significance and the joy of motivating, teaching and encouraging others. Making the assist has proven momentous for my soul. I give thanks to my soul mate – that big, round-headed, orange-complexioned, bouncy guy I fell in love with when I was five years old – for teaching me so many of God's truths on the court so that I might now be able to share life off of it with you.

I've often said, "The closer you get to the goal, the harder the foul. ™" I've certainly had my share of fouls. There have been so many times when I was so close to winning, yet I still wanted to quit. I've compassionately written this book because we have all experienced those moments. However, the fact that you are actually holding this book in your hands, years after I set out to write it, is as much a testimonial as it is good coaching advice – that you can always be a winner if you just stay committed to **Play Through the Foul!**

Best "Swishes!"

"Your passion is waiting for your courage to catch up."

- Marilyn Griest

PLAY THROUGH
THE FOUL

SOMETIMES...LIFE HURTS:
Know It's a Contact Sport

OFF THE COURT....

Untapped Potential

Standing just shy of 6' 2" with long, lanky arms and what most coaches would describe as a perfect basketball body for a woman, "Brenda" was the epitome of a highly-conditioned athlete. Although her outward physical appearance and style of dress were a little rough around the edges, she had a softness in her eyes that suggested femininity and maturity not yet realized but yearning to be discovered. Physically, she had tremendous athletic potential. But it was something about those eyes. As much of a star Brenda was proving to be on the court, off the court, those eyes had stories to tell....

I was in my first year of coaching at the University of Dayton (UD). Before I accepted the assistant coaching position, my superiors blatantly told me that in addition to my being knowledgeable and personable, my being an African American woman would help tremendously with the program's ability to recruit African American student-athletes.

"We need to recruit black kids. I'm a running style coach and I love pure athletes, especially athletic posts," my head coach explained. For those who don't know the basketball lingo, a "running style" coach is one who likes to play a fast-paced game. "Pure athletes" refers to lean, track runner-type athletes with seemingly raw or natural ability as opposed to a player who might have well-trained basketball skills but who appears mechanically trained. The underlying (and often controversial) connotation in the sports world is that the "pure athlete" term is more often used to describe a black player. "Posts" means post player –the position on a basketball team that primarily plays closest to the basket.

So although the coach's comment seemed a bit awkward at first, I was thankful there was no hidden agenda I would have to uncover on top of all my other duties. It was put to me plain and simple: Brenda fit the bill. Even with our knowledge of her struggle in the classroom and the possibility she might not cut it academically, she was one of our top recruiting priorities that year. She looked the athletic part, and she played the part even more.

I first met Brenda when she was a junior in high school on her unofficial visit to the UD campus. She had just finished running in a regional high school track meet. Known throughout the state as quite a sprinter, she was also a serious title contender in the shot put.

Brenda was relatively shy and wore a constant "deer in the headlights" stare with those big, soft, dark brown eyes. It was a little nerve-racking to talk to her. We would ask her a question and she'd stare for what seemed like an eternity, and then respond almost inaudibly. I'd crack a joke or two to lighten the mood (Coaching Staff Clown was always one of the unwritten duties I proudly performed). Again, she'd stare, and then almost as if waiting for permission, she'd place her hand over her mouth and giggle.

I remember conferring with one of the other assistants that she seemed socially retarded. We chalked it up to her nervousness and discomfort. After all, we were strangers standing around gazing at her like a pack of lions imagining a field of fresh, young antelope. Poor thing. She had no idea what she was getting into with all this college recruiting stuff. Sadly, we had no idea what we were getting into either.

Brenda and I got to know each other fairly well over the next couple of months of regular telephone calls and recruiting correspondence. Fortunately, we never had to worry about NCAA recruiting violations with Brenda. Division-I college coaches are permitted to initiate a specific and limited amount of phone calls to a prospective student-athlete, typically once per week. However, student-athletes are allowed to make as many phone calls as they like. This was Brenda's favorite recruiting rule, and she used it at any time of the day or night with the apparent expectation that each of the coaches on our staff was to drop what they were doing and entertain her. Generally, each of us did.

She seldom said a lot when she called, yet slowly but surely she began to open up. She seemed starved for attention, compassion and companionship. There seemed to be something about each member of our coaching staff that she trusted. My ability to relate to her as an African American woman allowed her the opportunity to be honest about a lot of things she admitted she didn't feel she could comfortably discuss with the other coaches, although she said she liked each of them a lot. So I guess there was some legitimacy to my head coach's declaration about my hiring, erasing my insecurities of being part of a relatively racially motivated scheme to capture the coveted "black athlete."

Shattered Truths

A few months after Brenda's visit I received a text message from our head coach. "Brenda verbally committed!" it read. I was thrilled but had reservations. Brenda would certainly help our program and was every bit of the long, lanky athlete our head coach desired. However, she was quite deficient academically and socially. And although I knew how much she could help us on the court, I wondered how much we would need to help her off of it.

Brenda was hiding a lot. I had no idea what, but being the communications type, I listened intently to the things she said as much as I did to the things she did not. She seemed to be full of contradictions. For example, when I would ask her about her grades, she'd tell me she was getting a B in English. Yet when I did some digging into her grades, I would find that she was in fact failing. I don't think she was a blatant or callous liar. I do believe, however, she was untruthful or vague about a lot of things, most likely driven by fear, confusion and even pain. No doubt, she had some serious issues.

By the end of Brenda's senior year of high school I had accepted a position with Indiana University. As thrilled as I was to be accepting a better position in a more competitive conference, as well as getting a huge raise and an opportunity to work with a familiar staff, it pained me to know I was leaving behind a great group of young women at UD. Additionally, our staff had aggressively recruited a group of student-athletes I had developed quite a rapport with but I would never have the opportunity to actually coach, especially Brenda, who I felt so much like a big sister and mentor to.

When I called her to break the news that I was leaving, she cried but said she understood. Then she was a bit silent and angry. She had trusted me to be there for her. I trusted myself to do the same. I explained to her that I would still be there for her, but from a distance. I told her she could still call me and talk to me about any and everything. I promised I'd be there.

Brenda took me up on my promise. One summer evening she called. She was attending summer school at UD and admitted she was having a difficult time staying focused. She explained to me she was on some sort of academic trial or probation. Her efforts and progress in summer school were critical to her being officially allowed to hold onto her scholarship offer. She told me she didn't think it was all going to work out. Her voice was dismal, distant and discouraged.

I chatted on with my usual optimistic advice that everything would work out if she tried harder, stayed focused and kept the faith. Brenda was silent, although I could hear a few faint sniffs through the phone receiver.

"It's some more to it than just school, Coach. Some kinda bad stuff has happened to me," Brenda slowly uttered.

"Like what?" I shot back, my sixth sense tingling like Spiderman's just before the Green Goblin is about to appear in the movies.

"It's got to do with my dad," she said.

I immediately flinched. I didn't know much, but I knew Brenda's father was a mess – a hot, garbage mess that the city refused to pick up!

First Impressions

I first met Brenda's father when they both made their official visit to UD during Brenda's senior year. He was chillin' in his own mind, in a hot, velvet or velour 1975-style red sweat suit and a stained white T-shirt. He was unshaven and wreaking of day-old alcohol. His eyes were fire-engine red. A smoker's stench greeted me long before he extended his arm to shake my hand.

I felt like my eyes were about to bleed!

He looked very angry because, well...he was! He believed Dayton was beneath his daughter's playing ability. After all, he had taught her everything she knew. That fact alone made her too good to play at a mid-major school in his mind. He believed she should go to Ohio State or any other big-named school that would take her.

He failed to realize she had far too many issues to have that happen. Most schools wouldn't touch her. We were as loyal and committed to Brenda as any school would ever be, and we were taking a huge risk to even try to get her in academically. She was very fortunate to have our interest. He would hear none of it.

Right away Brenda's father sized me up to see if I was one of those brain-washed black women taking the white man's side of things. I greeted him with my usual congenial and captivating smile and welcomed him to the arena. Our head coach had already learned from Brenda's high school coach that her father was allegedly an abusive drunk who disliked or distrusted "the white man" and was overly protective of his daughter. So Coach waited inside and allowed me to do the initial welcoming honors. Somewhat cowardly, but smart, I guess.

Brenda's dad didn't mix words. He actually came right out and said, "You should know right off the back (yes, he said "back" instead of "bat"), I ain't too happy about Brenda signing to play for y'all. I wanna know what Dayton can do for her, huh?"

Well, pleased to meet you too, Mr. Velour-clad, Soul Brotha Number 1001! I thought. I resisted the urge to answer him, thinking questions like these should be reserved for the head "white man in charge," if not out of protocol and respect, then certainly for the sake of my amusement of how this conversation was going to flow. I was never more pleased to NOT be the head coach than I was at this awkward, confrontational moment.

"The head coach is that little white dude, ain't he? Where are you from? You new here?" he asked.

"Yes, I am. This is actually my second year," I chimed back, feeling a rare opportunity to answer politely.

He continued, "Brenda didn't want me to come here today. She committed to y'all against my wishes. She knew I wanted her to go to Ohio State. But this is what she wanted so I hope she knows what she doing." Then he seemed to soften (if you can imagine that) and said, "I know she said she liked the coaches here a lot. That much I can say for y'all. Brenda really likes y'all. She need to play for people she can trust. That much I can say for why I think she wanted to come here."

I took that to be a positive and comfortable transition point, the best I thought I was going to get, and entered the building where I promptly introduced him to our head coach and the other assistants. Coach did what I thought was the best job he knew how of trying to be cordial and yet brave and unwavering on his beliefs about how Dayton was the best place for Brenda. Later I suggested we get some chicken wings from BW3s for lunch, which seemed to be of great pleasure to Brenda and her father.

Recruiting suggestion number one: always find out and then offer a recruit's favorite food if you want her visit to kick off right.

Over the next couple of hours, Brenda's dad seemed to mellow a bit, and she seemed to be more comfortable in a meeting she originally thought would surely lead to the Apocalypse. In the end, our coaching staff believed we did the best we could do with what we determined was the weirdest and most challenging parental recruiting visitation ever. But I will never forget Brenda's eyes. Although she always had a frightened innocence about her, around her father, she was even more reticent and borderline petrified. Come to think of it, even I was borderline petrified, and my eyes still ache even on memory recall of his visage.

Shocking Secrets

Those were the immediate thoughts that ran through my head upon hearing Brenda say, "It's got to do with my dad." My heart raced a little.

"He's in jail," she whispered.

"Okay," I said and then hesitated. "I'm sorry to hear that, baby, what happened?"

Brenda was silent. I thought she had hung up the phone. I was so afraid for her at this moment. I didn't know what to think, but I knew whatever she would say next was going to be bad. I was wrong. It was worse than bad....

"Bren? You there?"

"Yes ma'am," she answered. "He's in jail because of me." She began to cry.

"Brenda, did he hurt you? Are you all right? Please tell me what happened. Take your time. I'm here." I felt like I had just inhaled a golf ball.

Over the next hour, Brenda revealed to me what I still deem today as the saddest personal tragedy I have ever heard from anyone I had a personal connection with. Brenda's father had been sexually molesting and abusing her since she was 12 years old. Her mother and father separated when Brenda was younger, and she was left to her Mom's care with her sister and baby brother. A drug addict, Brenda's mom was on and off the streets and in and out of rehab constantly, many times leaving Brenda to care for her younger siblings alone.

As with so many of these scenarios, the children were neglected, malnourished and left to fend for themselves for food, shelter and guidance while their mother was searching for her next high. Eventually, when Brenda was 12, children's welfare services stepped in and a court placed them in the care of their father, which proved to be a case of tossing her from the frying pan to the fire.

Almost daily, Brenda's father used sex as a bargaining tool. He coerced and manipulated her by telling her if she didn't comply with his sexual wishes, he wouldn't let her go out with her friends, go to school or engage in any other "normal" childhood activity. Once he discovered how much she loved basketball, he used it as his trump card against her.

Brenda loved basketball more than any other player I've ever witnessed. Because she was talented, playing the game made her feel confident and accepted. Her hopes and dreams were vibrant when that ball was in her hands. It was her freedom, her security blanket, her ticket to stardom and a future free of molestation, abuse or pain.

Brenda told me no matter how many times she fought her father or cried or begged him to leave her alone, she always seemed to surrender when he threatened to take her basketball privileges away. As much as I have declared basketball has meant the world to me, it pales in comparison to what it obviously meant to Brenda.

The shocking truths Brenda had been hiding regarding her father's abuse, her mother's neglect, the real reason she found it difficult to concentrate or excel in school, and the ultimate physical and psychological trauma that lived for over five years behind those big, frightened eyes all came full disclosure in a private conversation one night to a young woman at the University of Dayton. Feeling she could no longer hold onto such guilty knowledge of such heinous crimes committed against Brenda, the young woman revealed the story to the head coach. He in turn notified the authorities.

Brenda's father's arrest and the subsequent battle of confessions and denials would soon play out in an Ohio courtroom. Meanwhile, as one could only expect under such extreme stress, Brenda failed to qualify academically at Dayton. She took refuge at a community college in another state to geographically distance herself from the madness, but also to try to keep her basketball dreams alive. She told me that playing basketball was the only way she kept from going completely crazy.

Another Setback

I was in my office at Indiana University when my India Arie (soul and R&B singer) ringtone began to chirp, "There's hope. It doesn't cost a thing to smile, you don't have to pay to laugh, you better thank God for that…" It always put me in a pleasant mood to hear those words no matter what kind of day I was having. I pleasantly answered with a sing-songy, "Hello, Coach Jones!"

There was silence, sniffing and then a faint voice. "Coach, it's me."

I knew it was Brenda. Suddenly my sixth sense told me I was about to hear something so depressing not even my favorite Arie song could pull me out. I rushed out of the office to find a private place to talk and better reception for my cell phone.

"What's the matter Bren?"

She answered softly, "My mom's been shot. She's in the hospital. They don't know if she's gonna make it!"

My heart sank a thousand times. I wanted to scream to the Heavens, "Dear God, why? How much does this poor girl have to endure?"

All I could say was, "Oh my God, Bren, I'm so, so sorry!"

"I'm sorry" seemed to be all I ever said to Brenda lately. She was down thirty with two minutes to play. What do you say to the team when you know they are down and defeated by all accounts? How do you say it's going to be okay when the championship is on the line and a blow out is inevitable? Every motivational basketball analogy I had ever used escaped me at this moment.

Brenda broke the silence with more alarming news. "They suspect my father was behind it. It was a drive-by. My mom recognized the shooter. She's in critical condition now though.

The bullet is lodged in her upper leg, like near her hip and they said they can't operate because removing it from the place it is stuck might kill her. They think my dad got some of his boys on the outside to go after her to keep her from testifying against him in court. They know my lawyer has been to see her and was going to put her on the stand. It's all my fault, Coach! I lost my dad and now I'm going to lose my Mom, too!"

For easily a minute in time, I stopped breathing. It was all so tragic. How could it all be real?

Brenda's story made local news and internet headlines during her trial once she finally agreed to testify in court against her father. Many times she would call me late at night to say she didn't think she could go on. Her accounts of how her father's attorney tried to make her look like a liar as her dad looked on with contempt, threatening with his eyes to have the last say in all of the courtroom madness, brought tears to my eyes. She kept asking me if she had done the right thing.

She said she decided to finally tell somebody because she just couldn't hold it in anymore. On her eighteenth birthday she knew she would be free from being legally under his care and he couldn't hold her hostage, trading her basketball wishes for his sexual desires. She felt her scholarship to college was her ticket out and she could get away from his molestation and abuse forever.

When Brenda arrived at Dayton for summer school, she found her body was free, but her mind was not. All those years of abuse haunted her daily. She recounted to me on the phone as she did again later at her trial, that her father had been making her "do bad things" three or four times a week if not more, since she was twelve years old, often in an alcoholic rage. She wondered how he could keep doing this to her and still say he loved her. Plus, he had a girlfriend! Why the hell couldn't he get what he needed from her?

Brenda told me her father would buy her a new pair of Jordan's or allow her to go out with friends as reward for her compliance and "good behavior." She finally got the nerve to use those Jordan's to kick him good and run away. She had escaped, or at least she thought. It didn't occur to her that she left behind a little sister. Was it her turn next? As the oldest sibling of three, she had always been the protector and provider. Who would protect them now? She had to tell someone. She had to testify, not just for her sake, but for what he might do to her sister.

He could be so vindictive and violent when he didn't get his way. Brenda constantly looked for rationale for her being the victim of such abuse. Then she searched for justification for being the snitch that would send her father to prison. She was so deeply lost in pain. I had no way to pull her out. All I could do was listen and pray.

My entire soul wept for Brenda. I never felt more helpless in my entire life and didn't think things could get any worse. Again, I was wrong.

Brenda's paternal grandmother took custody of her younger brother and sister. She banned Brenda from seeing them and blamed Brenda for her son being placed in prison. She maintained he was innocent and said Brenda was a dirty liar. She made it clear to Brenda to never try to contact her sister and brother while they were in her care.

This tore at Brenda in whatever feeling places she may have had left. Her heart was broken and she felt the world was against her. There seemed no relief in telling the truth, only additional pain and suffering. I would pray with her and try my hardest to encourage her. Nothing ever seemed to work.

A Second Chance

Finally, we were able to find one tiny shimmer of immunity from the madness around her: talking about basketball.

Brenda loved to hear my stories about the funny things that happened at our basketball practice, and she loved to tell me what was going on with her team. She always wanted to know what I thought she needed to work on to be a better player. We stopped talking so much about what was going on with the trial, her father's sentencing and her mother's battle with life, and instead we talked about her coach, her teammates and her potential to still play Division-I ball if she could dominate at the junior college level and get her academics together.

Brenda started playing so well that our head coach at Indiana eventually went out to see her play and to talk to her about recruiting considerations. Finally, Brenda and I were joyfully reunited when she made a trip to Indiana University to meet the team, visit the campus and size up the possibilities. This offered new hope and excitement I had never seen in Brenda.

We were overly cautious not to offer her false hope, however. That was the last thing she needed. We made it clear that her academics would have to improve dramatically. She seemed to embrace school and basketball with a new found passion. Undoubtedly she was still haunted by the chaos surrounding her personal life and all the unwanted press it had attracted, but she started receiving counseling, which she said was helping a little. Talking to me and to a few other trusted people was helping as well. Basketball, however, was helping a lot. It was and always had been her therapy of escape and hope.

Brenda was doing very well, and her junior college team was winning, most certainly a credit to her outstanding play. Her renewed optimism was a welcome sight, not just for her, but for all those in her corner. She was focused on being a winner again, at least for a little while.

Sometime mid-season I received a phone call from Brenda. Crying once again, she revealed to me that her mother had died from complications from the gunshot wound months earlier. She was devastated. Our staff sent grievance letters, which was very little consolation, but the best we could legally or legitimately do by NCAA rules. Additionally, it became very clear that Brenda wouldn't be able to qualify for admission to Indiana. We always knew she was a long shot, and even if she could qualify, her emotional and psychological struggles would always be difficult obstacles given the high demands of academic and athletic competitiveness.

I was left to tell her we could not accept her. The best we could do is to re-evaluate her in another year after she obtained her associate's degree. Although she was disappointed, she took the report like a woman who had become tremendously numb to bad news. She seemed to accept she was playing the game of life on a really sad and sorry losing team. Yet still, at least she was playing and she seemed to reason that was better than not playing at all. Or was it?

The Greatest Winner of All

In the March of 2007, my mother passed away. It was a very difficult time for me. Having only coached for a year at Indiana, I was left with little choice than to resign my position and return to Jacksonville, FL and look after my 80-year old father. I lost touch with a lot of people during that very trying time, including Brenda. By chance one day, however, I found myself wondering and worrying about her. Having lost my own mother now, I could only imagine what Brenda must have felt, particularly with all the other drama she had endured.

I called the two different cell phone numbers I had listed for Brenda in my contacts file. Both had been disconnected. I called around to a couple of places where I thought I could reach her. A mutual acquaintance advised me she had heard Brenda tried to commit suicide. My heart pounded through my chest at the news. I cried like a helpless baby. I had to find her. I had to know she was okay.

After finally getting a lead on her new cell number, I gathered myself with a deep breath and trusted God would lead me to her. The phone rang...

"Hello?" the voice faintly answered on the other end. It was Bren! Thank God she was alive!

"Brenda, it's me, Coach Jones," I said with a sigh of relief. "How you doing, kid?" I didn't want to let on I knew about her suicide attempt. I just wanted her to know I loved her and I cared about how she was doing.

In her usual soft spoken and cautious tone she replied, "I guess I'm alright, Coach. It's been a little rough though." I couldn't imagine her life being any rougher. I couldn't imagine anyone's life being so.

Brenda and I talked for at least an hour trying to catch up. I shared with her that I had been through some tough times myself, trying to overcome the sadness of my mother's death, but I was optimistic and I encouraged her to try to be the same in spite of all her trials. She admitted that she tried to take her own life. She said she had nothing else to believe in, nothing else to look forward to. Apologetically, she said she just lost it and she felt like she had no choice but to just give up.

I told her the fact she is still alive means God, our "Ultimate Coach," obviously had bigger plans, and a better position on the team for her. I told her she was the strongest person I think I ever met, even in her weakness. I told her what her story means to me, and what I thought it could one day mean to the world.

I told her that she is a *WINNER* on all accounts, because anyone else would likely have given up sooner.

I told her that she was allowed a *TURNOVER* or two having played the game of life so courageously.

Given the *FOULS* she had to play through, it was inevitable she might drop the ball every once in a while.

I told her she never failed to *REBOUND* for herself or for others.

She had made the necessary *ASSISTS* for her sister and brother.

No matter how tough things got, she remained *COACH-ABLE*, she *PLAYED WITH PASSION*, she *HANDLED* the *BALL*, and she had my utmost admiration for her ability to *STAY IN SHAPE* when so many times it was easier to just quit.

Brenda played this game of life in a way so few could or would, and I write this book in *APPLAUSE* of her courageous efforts to win despite the painfully dismal odds.

Finding Our Way

I've lost contact yet again with Brenda, but I think of her often. I pray for her and will never forget what she has meant to me in my growth and maturity in learning how difficult and seemingly unfair this game of life can truly be. Her story epitomizes in so many ways, perhaps to the extreme, how we are left with little choice but to courageously embrace adversity and play through life's fouls.

I always found it amazing that Brenda looked up to me. I wrote this book, in part, because I look up to her. I hope someday this book will find its way into her hands and that it might offer the kind of advice that will put a basketball spin on things so that she might understand it and benefit from it in the future.

Life truly is a contact sport, and sometimes those fouls really, really hurt. In the game of basketball, the fouls always seem to come most frequently and most painfully the closer you get to the goal. Life is just like that. But there's nothing worse than to discover you gave up right when you were so close to scoring that winning basket.

It takes courage, preparation, focus, finesse, faith and perseverance to play through the foul when you're driving hard toward the goal, trying to score that basket. What's great about the rules of the game is that even if you shoot for the goal and miss because you get fouled, there is a great chance you'll still get to step up to the free throw line. You'll shoot...you'll score... you'll win. It's a rule designed by God's grace. I believe that on the court and off. I hope you will believe it too, because when you get down to it, it's when we stop believing we can win that we're the most lost.

* * *

ON THE COURT....

Expect the Punches

"It's a contact sport. It's a lot of fun, but I wouldn't be doing my job as a Coach if I didn't tell you first and foremost, basketball is a contact sport. It's not tennis, golf or bowling. You'll have some challenges and you may even suffer a strained muscle or two in those sports, but in basketball you're also going to get hit, fouled, cheated and placed in painfully disadvantaged predicaments. Will you have what it takes to play through the fouls? It begins here," I pointed to my head, "and here in your heart. If you are going to be a winner on the court and if you are going to be a winner the rest of your life off of it, you have to know up front that you are playing a contact sport."

That's the way my hard-driven basketball lectures usually began. I believe you should eat the stuff you don't like so much first, that way dessert always tastes sweeter. That's my approach to most things, both in basketball and in life.

A pastor once told me the greatest trick the devil uses against us is to convince us he doesn't exist. So we live our lives not expecting the trials that surely come and we react surprised, bewildered, confused and horrified. It takes us longer to get over the abuse, the cheating, the lies and the flagrant fouls in our lives because we spend so much time contemplating why on earth these horrible things could happen to us. Some of us even throw pity parties and invite our friends to join in.

I'm in no way saying you are not allowed to react with sadness or express the pain you are feeling. You must. It's only natural. I am saying one of the first steps in recovering, rehabbing and healing, or reducing the initial shock to the pain is to accept in life there is always going to be good and evil and we are not going to understand all things.

At the very least, understand life is not always going to be easy, because the devil does exist. He is your opponent. He is God's opponent, and if you are playing for God's team, then you must listen to your Coach!

Plan for the Foul

I always told my players right away, before they stepped onto the court to participate in the first lay-up line, the first free throw shooting drill, the first on-court sprints, that they had to be mentally tough and they had to expect they are going to get fouled. They had to know the game is going to be exhilarating and competitively fun most of the time, but it is going to be emotionally draining and physically demanding as well.

As their coach, I expected them to listen to me and I expected them to trust my judgment. I didn't need a bunch of mini-coaches; I needed a bunch of committed, determined, mentally tough players who understood that when they are driving through the lane to score that basket, they should not flinch or throw up a wild shot because they are afraid they will get fouled. I definitely didn't want players afraid to play at all for fear getting hurt. That would be like inviting the opponent to win.

From a position of physical and mental strength, they had to expect that they would get fouled first. Only then could they see that they had the opportunity to score if they stayed strong and focused, and that they even got extra points on the "and one" free throw opportunities that would follow.

When we think of contact in terms of sports, we generally think of the slapping, hacking, tripping or shoving that goes on during the game. However, it's often the little elements of contact that bother us even more. I remember coaching a young girl's team at a summer basketball camp. I called a much needed time-out and noticed one of my young players coming out of the game red-faced, fighting back tears and in a huge huff.

"What is it, Melissa?" I asked. "Why do you look so frustrated?"

"That big girl keeps flicking her hair and getting her sweat on me!" she howled back.

I couldn't help but laugh. However, this was a real concern for little Melissa. She really didn't want to get someone else's sweat on her. And I can't say I blamed her. Wearing someone else's sweat is definitely on my "Top Ten Things That Gross Me Out" list! It's a close tie with having some guy's chewed food inadvertently fly out his mouth and find a landing spot on my forehead!

"Basketball is a contact sport. Players sweat. That's just the way it is," I tried to reason with Melissa, who now had her arms folded, lips poked out and eyes piercing through me. She would have none of it. She did not want to go back in the game. She matter-of-factly announced she needed a sub, grabbed her towel and water bottle, sat down on the floor at the end of our court-side position and cried for the next five minutes.

Granted, Melissa was only nine or ten years old, but grown adults give up or get flustered in the same way. We know that when we decide to play a game where other people are sweating we run the risk of coming into unwanted contact with their per-spiration. Yet when the first drop of sweat touches us, we react as if it is some big unwelcome surprise and suddenly it's too much too handle. I suspect that many people who react this way are a lot like Melissa in their experiences.

Melissa's basketball experience was limited to her driveway in suburbia, with mom or dad or a few friends not exerting very much energy or physical contact. Her experience had been slight, and so was her mindset and her heart. If your life experiences are limited to friendly non-contact shooting games, you are in for some contact culture shock, my friend, once you competitively start playing in a real game. Whoever told you life would be simple or that you are likely to coast through because you are somehow above the opposition and

thus exempt from unwanted contact is a liar. Please trust me
on this one.

It's Physical...And Mental

Contact is not always just going to be about sweat and fouls,
either. How about the name calling and trash talk? How will
you handle that? Trash talk and verbal slurs aren't limited to the
tatted, street-ball thug you may have stereotypically conjured up
in your mind. People you believe to be your closest friends and
likely a few choice family members are dogging you out right
now. If they're not, eventually someone will. If you've ever been
talked down to, called horrible names, lied to or had rumors
spread about you, you know there are times when it hurts far
worse than getting smacked a time or two. The pain doubles
when it's someone you are close to.

When my big brother, two years my elder, was eleven, he called
me names they hadn't even made up yet. Growing up outside of
Washington, DC, we went at it daily as I was trying to challenge
him playing ball in the driveway. Sometimes he could rattle off
about five or six adjectives at once like, "You ugly, big-headed,
fat, smelly, big nosed, stupid sucker!" All the while he'd be trying
to pummel his entire body through me, elbow first, while driving
to the basket.

Admittedly, sometimes I'd cry, but as I matured and continued
to challenge him, not only was I throwing a few elbows of my
own, but having won my grade school spelling and vocabulary
bee, I was also able to rattle off some hurtful adjectives myself!
I'm not saying this was always the right thing to do, as a few
times my mouth tried to write checks my butt couldn't cash. I
am saying it is the tough thing sometimes you have to do. (This
is the part of the book where I thank my verbally and sometimes
physically abusive brother for making me tough and letting me
know very early on that basketball and life are contact sports.)

Playing any game has always been easier when I went in

knowing that not everyone will play fair, names will be called, sweat might fly, and sometimes there will even be elbows, kicks, body blows and punches. It all seemed to hurt a bit less when I didn't set up the expectation that the opposition would just let me shoot and score because I'm such a nice person.

As a coach, I've learned that the best thing I can do is not necessarily teach a skill, but rather cultivate a mindset. So understand this if you can't grasp anything else: It's a contact sport you're playing. While it is impossible to not occasionally be disappointed with the perceivably unfair way the game is played and the amount of unwanted contact we receive at times, knowing and accepting in advance that this is just the way the opponent comes at us as part of the game certainly helps us overcome things quicker.

It is up to us to do our best and to do whatever is necessary to position ourselves in strength, mentally, physically and spiritually. When the contact becomes too much to bear, we find faith in our Ultimate Coach to get us through the battle and ultimately win the game.

THE POWER OF PERSEVERANCE:
Get in Shape, Stay in Shape

OFF THE COURT....

The First Step

I was undertaking a tough and ugly job, but I had to do it. If I didn't, who would? No fitness center, personal trainer, nor work-out DVD would suffice. It was time for me to be accountable.

"No one forced me to eat the four helpings of barbecue ribs, two pieces of chicken, pint of molasses-loaded baked beans, three bratwursts, two cheeseburgers and that sinful mound of strawberry shortcake at my last cookout. For Heaven's sake, did my guests even get anything to eat? Uh-oh! Had I unknowingly eaten one of my guests?" I disgustedly wondered aloud.

I had considered myself a professional eater for a long time. In fact, I was a self-proclaimed expert at it. The reality finally hit that I had been taking that job far too seriously. I was chronically overworked and the stress was taking a serious toll on my body, to the tune of 30 unwelcomed pounds around my midsection, backside and hips. It was time to undertake that painful process I had gone through so many times before that

I affectionately named, "Get my fat butt in shape."

I woke up Sunday morning and decided to begin that routine I had begun too many times to count... and had quit too many more over the past two decades. Each time I endured the agony of sore muscles and aching knees and back, I vowed that once I got into shape, I would never allow myself to get back out. I would never allow myself to eat unhealthily and gain all that weight back. I would never again step onto the scale and try to convince myself it must be broken because the counter was off by at least 25 pounds. "This time, I will remain fit for life!" I'd exclaim to anyone who cared to listen. (I hadn't noticed that no one cared to listen anymore.)

This morning, I hoped that God was listening. That's why I started on a Sunday. It just made it seem more official and divine. Surely this would help me through the pain and agony that was about to come.

Dressed in my white cut-off T-shirt, baggy Indiana Hoosiers red gym shorts and a brand new matching red bandana tied around my head, I stepped outside into the fresh morning air. I placed my sunglasses on my face, more out of vanity to look cool than to actually protect me from the sun's UV rays. I thought looking cool – as if I actually enjoyed working out – would be great motivational psychology. I also figured those cool specs would mask the tears running down my face and hide the agony in my eyes.

Armed with my iPod and favorite inspirational tunes, I headed out for a four-mile speed walk through my beautiful Jacksonville, FL community. I told myself to get started earlier tomorrow, as it was already a very uncomfortable 83 degrees at just 10:30 a.m.

Time to Kick It Up a Notch

After the first mile of walking, I was already feeling like I was suffering from a bit of heat exhaustion. My natural honey-caramel skin tone had already turned five shades darker to a Tootsie Roll chocolate complexion. I grabbed the end of my white T-shirt to wipe the perspiration that was beginning to pour into my eyes. When I looked down at my shirt I was alarmed to see it was stained bright red!

"Oh my God, I'm bleeding! But I haven't been cut! I'm bleeding right out of my pores!" I shrieked. I'd never seen any medical condition like this, even on my favorite television show House. I was sweating blood! I thought "sweating blood" was only a metaphor, not something humanly possible!

Just as I was about to flag someone down to call 911 and get me to a hospital emergency room, I realized the wet, red stain on my shirt was the dye seeping from my brand new red bandana.

"You big, over-dramatic dummy," I chuckled to myself. "All you've done is walked a mile and already you think you're dying from some rare heat-induced blood perspiration! Stop being a wimp, Vera! Get a grip."

I decided it was time to pick up the pace. I had a whopping 30 pounds to lose. There was no time for walking. I needed to push myself. I hadn't attempted to jog in a good nine months, but I couldn't let that stop me from challenging myself with a little cardiovascular assertiveness.

Two minutes into my run, just up ahead on the running trail, I spotted a frail looking little old lady, mid-sixtyish, who couldn't have been more than 5'2" and 110 pounds. In my typical competitive spirit, I immediately challenged myself to increase my pace enough to catch up to her within the next minute, and then use my impressive gait and stamina to pass her, leaving her in my dust yearning for my youthful athleticism and energy. Surely that would be easy enough.

The minute came and went, and although I had gained ground, I still hadn't caught up to that little old woman.

"What the heck did she have for breakfast, oatmeal and jet fuel? She must be a former Olympian or something," I reasoned to myself.

I was searching for any excuse to keep me from being discouraged. I'd never been much of a pure runner. Unless I had a basketball in my hand, I just wasn't interested in moving my feet quickly and getting out of breath. In college I could be counted on to be dead last in our regular 1.5 mile runs. My coach would clock everyone else with a stopwatch. With me, she'd use a calendar! Still, I could at least run in short bursts pretty quickly. I passionately believed there was no reason why I couldn't catch this woman.

I was five minutes into the whole running thing and I was still behind her. Not only that, but my left knee was starting to shout obscenities at me while my lower back was crying and threatening to marshal the rest of my body parts into a full-fledged revolt. "Mind over matter," the optimist in me kept saying to myself. "You can do it!"

"Do what!" the antagonist part of my brain answered back. "Collapse in this hot sun and have a heart attack?"

I decided the little old woman was definitely a former Olympian and it was best if I just kept to my own pace instead of trying to keep up with her. After all, it was only my first day. I needed to be less demanding and more positive because everything about me wanted to quit and I hadn't even run a half mile yet!

Just then I heard this rhythmic clapping sound. I thought it was from my iPod, but it was off beat from the melody of the song.

"What on earth could that be? It sounds almost like someone is clapping for me, cheering me on. But where are they?" I queried. I kept running and began to look around but didn't see anyone. Still the clapping sound remained. I was convinced someone was cheering me on and I had to know who it was so I could wave, smile and thank them for their encouragement.

I took my earphones off and kept listening as I ran. "Clap.... clap....clap...clap." It was louder, steady and very rhythmic. Was it one of the construction vehicles up ahead? Was it the weed whacker the lawn maintenance guy was using? "Clap....clap.... clap....clap...." It continued.

My curiosity got the better of me, so I stopped running and looked around. I saw and heard nothing more as I huffed and puffed and wheezed. Once I gathered my breath, I decided to pop my headphones on and began running again. Immediately the clapping returned.

"Holy cow!" I exclaimed in revelation. "No one is cheering for me!" My discovery was shocking. The peculiar clapping noise was self-generated – it was the sound of my butt cheeks and thighs slamming together as I ran. I had gotten so fat and out of shape that I had turned my aerobic run into a percussion mini-concert! The revelation disgusted me, discouraged me then sent me into shameful laughter at myself.

Combined with the heat exhaustion, "bloody sweat" and em-barrassment of being outrun by a woman from the local geriatric center, I decided to end my run for the day. I couldn't take myself seriously anymore. I thought it would be best just to stick to the speed walk I started out with – that at least would be less strenuous, not to mention a heck of a lot more silent.

Getting to the Skinny of It

Day one of getting in shape ended with the completion of my intended four miles, and a Vera that was drenched in sweat, winded, weak and deeply tanned. It was ugly, but it was a start. I knew I was a long way from my goal, but this time, I was more determined than ever to maintain a healthy lifestyle.

My mother had recently passed away, having spent a lifetime suffering from many ills. Diabetes, high blood pressure and cancer all run in my family. I did not want to become the latest statistic, nor was I interested in looking in the mirror and seeing someone I wasn't proud of physically. I'd been a collegiate athlete and a coach. I knew what it took to push myself, and I was well aware of the painful persistence required to get into shape. I was prepared to get there. Where I always seemed to fall short was in maintaining the discipline it took to stay in shape.

When I woke up on day two, my legs, shoulder, back, chest and arms all begged me to go back to sleep. I reminded myself of my lack of discipline in the past and how frustrated I had been the morning before when I stepped on that scale. There was no way around it. I had to get back out there and go for it.

Today, I would opt for an already washed bandana so I wouldn't have any unnecessary blood-sweat anxiety attacks. I would push myself but also pace myself to maximize my workout. I would follow a high protein diet, eat lots of salads and drink lots of water. I would add in some abdominal exercises, lunges and push-ups to build muscle tone. I would be better today in every way, mentally, physically and spiritually.

"I can and I will do all of these things!" I asserted, "If I could just get out of this darn bed!"

Every morning for the first week, my mind and body wrestled this way. Nonetheless, my mind always won. By week two, I felt a little stronger and had even dropped five pounds! I was on my way. I still had many days that I just could not bring myself to workout. So I made a pact that as long as I got in five days a week and never allowed myself to go two consecutive days without some form of aerobic activity, I would be satisfied.

Before long I found that I actually enjoyed my walks and I had gradually worked my way into interval running. Two months later, I was passing "Olympic Grandma" easily! I felt strong and proud. I'd lost 15 pounds and it showed. I started allowing myself to have "cheat" days, but I at least kept the four helpings of barbecue ribs to two.

A year had gone by before I realized that I was still working out according to plan. At times I found myself hopping on and off that weight rollercoaster ride, because I would still overdo it with my eating fetish (a pig can't change her snout), but I was overdoing it a lot less. The one thing I kept as part of my lifestyle was consistently getting exercise. I felt very fit and realized I hadn't gotten sick the entire year. I became well-known in my neighborhood. I'd get daily horn toots and waves from neighbors on their way to work. Some of them even would stop to tell me how much they admired my diligence and persistence. A couple of ladies even stopped to ask if they could train with me sometimes.

How about that...people really were cheering for me now. This was great, because since I dropped twenty pounds I could no longer generate my own shameful body clapping. The value of my working out had extended long past my personal pride and physical improvement. It had become an encouragement to others. It wasn't like I was a great marathon runner or fitness star. I was just a regular old 40-something chick determined to get her physical groove back.

The Payoff

My greatest revelation of the value of getting into shape and then staying there was still yet to be realized. A year after I began my fitness quest, I moved to a new neighborhood. Excited to see the homes in the community and chart out a new route for my fitness walks and runs, I headed down the main street in my sub-development. As I walked past one of the homes, I noticed the garage door was up. There was a large black SUV in the driveway. Unbeknown to me, on the other side of that SUV was a matching large black Rottweiler!

A deep-throated "Roo-roo-roo-roo-roof!" echoed in my ears from this gigantic, ferocious animal that sounded like he was the vocal prodigy of Barry White and Darth Vader. Every hair on my body stood on end. It felt like my spine sent an electrical shock up into my heart, throat and eyes while simultaneously running through my bladder and down into my knees!

With the barking Cujo-the-killer-dog beast on the chase, I took off running in a world-record breaking sprint past at least ten houses before I dared to look back. I promise you I had never run so fast in my entire life!

The Rottweiler must have been on a long chain, because when I did gather up the courage to look back over my shoulder, he was sniffing around in the grass in his front yard. He seemed to have a smirk on his face like, "Hah, hah, hah! Did you see how fast she ran? I terrified another one! I still got it!"

I took it upon myself to feel pretty proud too, even in my hysteria.

"Wow! Did you see how big that monster was? I can't believe how fast I got away! Thank God I'm in shape! I'm not even tired. I think I might have peed on myself, but I'm not tired! Whew, you go girl!"

In the midst of this ridiculously haughty celebration, my heart was still pounding through my chest from the big black Rottweiler scare. That's when I looked down on the sidewalk, only to see a big black snake two steps in front of me! Expletives of the triple-X kind screeched out my mouth. I straddle-leaped into the air at what felt like the length and height of a stretch limousine. I was sure I heard the bionic sound effects of Steve Austin, the Six-Million Dollar Man, ring out from my loins when I finally reconnected with the sidewalk.

It felt like fire ants were engulfing my entire body as I shook in fear and disbelief. A huge black Rottweiler at my back, and then a four-foot black snake underfoot? Surely there must have been a black cloud overhead! Was there a "Scare Vera to Death" holiday I didn't know about?

My heart was racing and before I knew it I was crying....no I was laughing....no, crying. I'm not sure what kind of schizo-phrenic, out-of-body fit I was experiencing, but in the midst of it, I was still marveling at how in shape I was.

"A lesser being would have had a coronary right there on the spot, likely just from the dog. But I endured the dog and the snake, back-to-back! How many other people can honestly say they could survive that madness? I've got to put this in a book!"

As I continued down the street in my hysterically motivated self-glorification, a very important yet disturbing thought occurred to me. This street in my lovely, new, dog and snake infested neighborhood ended in a cul-de-sac. I was at a dead end. There was no other way home but to turn around and walk back up the way I came down.

"Are you kidding me?" I screamed out loud to no one listening. I didn't have a cell phone to call anyone to come get me. I didn't know any of my new neighbors, and if I did the smelly mix of fear and sweat tainting my entire body was truly a bad introductory look for me. I knew I could likely avoid the snake if I walked on the other side of the street, provided it had not slithered over there to maniacally outwit me already. But what about the dog? What if he wasn't on a chain? I never really stopped to see. In all of this madness, I realized I had but one thing on my side beyond my faith: I had finally gotten in shape and stayed that way. I could make it past "Cujo."

It would be a tough and ugly job, but I had to do it!

* * *

ON THE COURT:

Preparation is Key

Most of us are not fitness fanatics. However, many of us enjoy athletic participation or active lifestyles. Virtually everyone understands the need to be in great shape, yet few possess the grit, determination and discipline required to be at the top of their physical game.

I don't suggest that we all run to the nearest boot camp or Olympic training facility to train for and win the gold. The getting in shape and staying in shape I refer to here is as much about mental preparation as it is physical. In the game of life, you will always have to identify the level or quality of life you want. Some people will aspire to be the next Oprah Winfrey, Bill Gates, Michael Jordan or President of the United States, but you don't have to set your sights that high to be happy, successful and fulfilled. Choosing to play at a high level will most certainly require a great deal of conditioning. American's most prominent and successful icons will tell you their successes didn't come without some serious commitment, dedication and perseverance. This is what "being in shape" is all about.

No matter what your chosen profession or field of endeavor, if you are looking to gain position, favor or title, you will need to be in shape to perform whatever tasks are required. Why? Because life is a contact sport. It' a game you are most likely to win and enjoy when you are best prepared.

Basketball players get hit all the time. They have defenders breathing down their necks and taunting their faces. Sweat runs into their eyes and onto each other as they run and jump. They bump constantly, and yet most play the game without really noticing how often or how hard they've been hit.

Experience has taught players this is naturally part of the game, so they have trained for it. Sure, some players pout and ride the referees, usually to no avail, but most of the time, they play the game at a tempo and physicality so intense it has come to be accepted and even revered. Thus, it stands to reason that the training required to play the game effectively would need to be as intense. Players who are in the kind of shape to endure the contact have far greater time enjoying the game than those who waste all the fun counting hits and placing blame.

The game of life, like basketball, comes complete with challenges, obstacles, opponents, surprise attacks, pressure and fouls, all requiring a need for mental toughness, strategy, finesse, strength and endurance. Therefore, you have to practice your craft or skill. You have to train for your job or position. You have to truly apply yourself and prepare yourself to overcome obstacles, whatever they may be, wherever they may come from.

You may not have a clue what specific kind of challenge awaits you, but your confidence combined with your ability to react with the mental fortitude, physical agility or emotional finesse you've gained from your practice or training is often the difference in your favorable outcome of the game. Best said you must work out if you want to work up.

Know Your Goal

As silly as the illustration of being chased by a Rottweiler may seem, it has tremendous significance when you look at the daily little things that happen in life to challenge us unexpectedly. If my predicament were a basketball game, that Rottweiler and snake were my opponents that double teamed me when I was least aware. I had to think quickly to figure out what to do (although running like a madwoman was likely more of an inbred flight response than a marvelous strategy on my part.)

What's significant here is I had to move quickly to physically change my speed or direction to avoid that dog-snake trap. If it had been a year earlier, I probably wouldn't have been able to move at all. My heart might not have withstood the fear or the flight. My mind may have said, "Run!" but my body would have said, "No sir, Sister, can't do. Let's just sit here and scream and pray Cujo already had breakfast."

When faced with an unexpected and even fearful challenge, I felt a surge of confidence that I would beat the odds in spite of my fear. I could make it through this adverse experience, no matter how physically threatening because my mind had been conditioned to be resilient. I was experiencing the truth of the adage that "tough times don't last, tough people do."

What are you doing in your everyday life to get in shape and stay in shape? What is your goal? Are you hoping to obtain a job promotion? If so, are you going above and beyond your competition or putting in the quality work to be recognized? Do you maintain this high level of performance consistently? Everyone is capable of doing a great job once in a while. The real office superstar works smarter and harder to perform a great job regularly without very many "cheat days." Peers recognize the superstar as someone who is always getting the job done. They may even be cheering for you like my neighbors honking their horns when I was out on my run. They cheer for you because they admire your hard work and persistence.

No doubt, there will be some maladjusted individuals who will envy rather than admire your diligence and success. Even this will be a reflection of the greatness you have achieved. Haters are the devil's way of complaining, "Darn, he or she is winning and I'm not!" Nonetheless, you are truly at the top of your game when your work ethic inspires and encourages others to raise their performances. You become a leader by example. Now it's not just about your being the star, but your whole team being on top of the game.

Have you ever watched a basketball game and seen a guy dive on the floor after a loose ball? There is no grittier teammate than one who is willing to risk injury by diving on a hardwood floor determined to secure that basketball for his team. Suddenly that selfless act of dedication and desire inspires another teammate to dive down too. Before long there's a pile of sweaty, determined people heaped up in feisty determination.

Teammates on the bench are screaming and cheering, and the fans start going wild! When the play is over and possession secured, the other players that didn't hit the deck rush over to help their teammates up, high-fiving, chest bumping, fist pounding one another with snarls of admiration and appreciation all over their faces. The emotion is electric and contagious because one guy decided to dive for the ball.

I love that kind of blue collar player. He understands the value of getting in shape and staying in shape. Face it. You are a lot less likely to exert extra energy to do anything if you know you are out of shape. However, that guy has trained hard so consistently there's no fear or hesitation with him anymore. He takes risks, gives the extra effort, dives in and dives after the little successes in the game to gain even the slightest edge. He doesn't have to be the most athletic, nor the smartest. He's just determined to outwork everybody. We love that guy on our team!

There are a few times when life is like hitting a half-court shot as the buzzer sounds – sometimes you just get lucky. Far more often, however, it isn't luck, but preparation that wins the game. In countless interviews with players who have just won a championship game or a big contest I have heard them express, "This is what we trained so hard for. This makes all those hours of practice, training and conditioning worth it."

Oddly enough, the players on those teams aren't practicing big, lucky half court shots very often or very seriously. They could, but since that shot is a "long shot" literally, they prepare for it only as such. Instead, teams focus more regularly on practicing the little things: endurance drills, offensive and defensive positioning, ball handling, passing, shooting techniques and even how to take a charge.

For those of you non-basketball folks, taking a charge means positioning yourself in front of a moving offensive player and falling backwards when contact is made via his or her forward motion into your motionless body. It is purposely putting yourself in the line of contact (and usually pain) to cause an offensive foul and regain possession of the ball for your team.

As kamikaze as this tactic sounds, it is a part of the game and something good teams practice. If you don't know how to take this hit, you risk broken wrists, a bruised chest and a very sore backside. I've never known anyone who actually enjoyed repetitive drills of getting plowed over and bouncing off his or her derrière underneath the basket, especially since taking a charge is not a part of the game that happens very often. Yet it is a little aspect of a game that could cause a big momentum swing in a team's favor when it does occur. So you have to be ready.

It is also very important to understand that as demanding as any kind of training or conditioning can be, getting proper rest is crucial to achieving the results you wish. On the court, a coach has to know when to call time-out to give the team a rest. No matter how good the best player is, even he or she will need a substitution at some point – a chance to towel off, rest the muscles, breathe and mentally regroup for the next intense moment of the game.

Know that it is not only acceptable, but a necessity to be still sometimes. Anxiety and stress are counterproductive to all things we seek to achieve. Rest combats these ills. Getting in shape and staying there lies in a delicate balance of knowing when you are reasonably pushing yourself and when you are pushing yourself beyond reason.

I've been in basketball practices where overzealous coaches failed to realize they were pushing their athletes too hard and ended up with a team full of player injuries or a tired team unable to perform at its maximum potential on game day. Lack of proper rest is dreadfully evident everywhere these days: overly aggressive athletes tear ligaments and strain muscles; ambitious singers overwork their vocal cords; over-taxed construction workers throw their backs out; overworked typists get carpal tunnel strains; overworked computer users suffer from impaired eyesight; exhausted truck drivers cause accidents.

Once, I set out to do 300 abdominal crunches a day continuously and ended up having hernia surgery six months later. You have to know the setbacks that will accompany your overexertion or malpractice before you embark on intense training and allow wisdom to be your guide to rest properly. In my getting in shape example earlier, I knew setting up the expectation to walk or run every day was setting me up for failure. Having long celebrated my 40th birthday and having body parts that actually made noises, I thought five days a week was a good rule. It beat the zero days a week I had been used to by a long shot.

It is said that God created all things in the heavens and the universe in six days and on the seventh He rested. I doubt seriously He ever once said, "I really should have pushed myself that last day. Rest is for wimps."

Take Your Best Shot

So it is with virtually every endeavor in which we desire to gain or triumph beyond what we have already achieved:

- We work to strengthen ourselves and we grow from the different experiences that cause us to exert our energy.

- We rest to regain our energy as we meditate and contemplate our plans, goals, and desires.

- We play because there is joy in even the little victories in the game of life.

That joy is maximized when we are most prepared. The game is full of adversity and surprises, big, small and in between. Determine your goal. Then be honest with how prepared you are to meet that goal. If you discover you fall short of being at your best, then it is time for you to make the commitment to get into shape.

Know up front that if getting into shape comes too easily, you probably aren't doing it right. There is a reason we use the term "growing pains." Once you've grown into shape, be determined and disciplined to stay there. This means your training never stops, and likely intensifies if you are truly seeking results to become a more skilled or more prepared player in the game.

Finally, no one wants to work hard at a goal and never reap the benefits or celebrate the victory, just as no basketball team ever wants to train hard for months of practice only to lose every game all season. You have to play the game with the mentality that you will win, not with the mentality that you are afraid to lose. Getting the extra training, challenging yourself mentally and physically, putting in the extra effort to perfect the little things, and regularly testing your endurance will put you ahead of the game.

For as long as there is one more game to play, your training and conditioning will never be in vain. There will never be failure associated with knowing you're better, stronger, faster or wiser than before. The more in shape you are, the harder it will always be for those "dog days" to jump out and bite you unexpectedly, or for that snake in the grass to intimidate you away from your chosen path. So shape up! Your faith and your confidence will sustain you. Ultimately, in one way or another, you will win.

GAIN A NEW PERSPECTIVE:
Be Coachable

OFF THE COURT....

A Life-Changing Moment

"You're not a WNBA player, you're not a WNBA Coach, and in fact, you haven't coached at all on the college level. You were a good player in the 80s. It's 2003. I'm not saying you're not a good analyst; I just believe our broadcast needs a WNBA face or a more credible 'big name' if we want to grow our brand. ESPN is the face of women's basketball. We need a face that people will know. We just need to move in a different direction..."

I remember those words like they were spoken five minutes ago. They came from a young woman executive who was hired to replace ESPN's top guy in charge of NCAA Women's Basketball Programming. After working with The Worldwide Leader In Sports for seven seasons as a basketball Color Analyst on NCAA and WNBA broadcasts, three of which included the celebrated Road To The Final Four studio telecasts, I was told that my contract was not going to be renewed, mostly because I wasn't a young or famous WNBA player or college coach.

But I was a loyal, dedicated broadcaster. I thought surely that should count for something. In what seemed to have occurred in the blink of an eye, I had risen to a low-name or no-name behind the scenes commentator to part of the NCAA Women's Basketball Final Four studio team. My "job" was to sit next to Robin Roberts, one of my longtime broadcasting idols, and talk about the game I had loved and been around since I learned to spell my name. And I was paid handsomely to do it! That wasn't a job to me. That was paradise!

The executive producer who auditioned me three years earlier and brought me on board for the Final Four studio show told me I was chosen because he loved that I brought wit and personality to the broadcast. He loved the fact that I was knowledgeable but could put a layman's spin on the game. He said I had a likeability that made people feel comfortable, like they were sitting across a table talking and having a cup of coffee with their sister.

Turns out one man's hot, tasty cup of coffee was another woman's bitter coffee grinds. That hot coffee got thrown in my face and burned through to my soul! While the young woman producer basically shared she would not be renewing my contract to return as a Final Four studio analyst, she did say she was sure they could "find some games for me to do."

Let me explain something. When you have comfortably been living for three years on the security of a six-figure contract, and then the reality hits that you have been reduced to "some games to do" without a contract, you feel like Satan himself just put the pitchfork through your heart and your finances.

I was a single mother! How on earth was I supposed to go from the proverbial broadcasting mountain top to the Valley of Broke, with no advance warning? I was forced to swallow this horrible reality only two weeks before my contract ended. And why was this happening again? Oh, because I wasn't in the WNBA? Well newsflash, there was no chance I was ever going to be in the WNBA. It wasn't even an option 15 years ago when I had finished my college career. But I had been around the game of basketball as a broadcaster all 15 of those years, so surely that had to be worth something.

To counter that argument, "Little Ms. ESPN Executive Producer" added that she thought there were times when my sideline reporting needed improvement and my analysis and delivery needed to be tighter and more insightful, with less humor. She said she believed there were advantages of having played or coached recently that would have helped my insight. The game was changing.

You wouldn't know the changes in the game of basketball let alone good humor if they slapped you in the face! I smugly thought to myself. My blood was boiling so I was really high on the "slap you in the face" part! I believed her criticisms were concocted defensively because inside I knew I was a good and popular broadcaster. I felt she was looking for justifications for not having me return.

Yet, it was just a few months earlier that I had sat in her office and asked her for a critique of my work. Since she was the new boss, I wanted to be sure my work met her expectations. During this meeting I asked her for her constructive criticism and she told me, "I really can't think of one thing to share with you. I thought the broadcasts were awesome! I've heard nothing but good things. We had some of the highest ratings for women's basketball programming ever. I would really have to sit down and watch film again to come up with what I feel you need to work on. I just think you do a great job and you're a valuable member of our team. I'm looking forward to working with you."

I reminded her of this little conversation we previously shared and suggested that if she thought my work had slipped since that "Vera is awesome" conversation, why didn't she tell me when I had a chance to make adjustments? She agreed my argument was valid and that she might have dropped the ball with me in this regard.

It became clear that the decision to "move in a different direction" was as pre-meditated as it was inevitable. My 37-year-old eyes watched as a 23-year-old blonde fresh out of college replaced me. Was she more experienced? No. But she was about to become a WNBA name. She was young, she was attractive, and she had a lot of potential. She was that new, young face they could mold and brand into a women's basketball television celebrity, which is what the new producer basically told me she wanted.

She made it clear that Robin Roberts and I were part of the previous producer's vision. Now that Robin was about to move on to ABC's *Good Morning America*, what the heck did she need me for? After all, I wasn't a coach, I wasn't a big name, I wasn't a WNBA star, and oh yeah, I hadn't played basketball since the Jheri Curl was in style. Truth be told, I had one of those drippy hairdos in the 80s! In the face of that reality, I was painfully beginning to see I definitely didn't fit her vision, and it mattered little what my personal circumstances or opinions were. That's the way the professional ball bounces. Game over, thanks for playing....Next!

Poor, Poor Me

So what was I going to do now? I had a dream and a plan to spend the next five years honing my broadcast talent and visibility so that I could readily step in once Oprah retired! I suspect I could have continued in the direction of pursuing that dream, just under different circumstances than I had anticipated if I was willing to be flexible and work harder. Instead, I chose to have a pity party and pout. I didn't pout for a week or two. I pouted for a year and a half! Although my agent was more than ready to line up new broadcasting opportunities, somewhere I just lost the passion to continue.

National television had proven to be a very superficial, political disappointment for me. My mind was constantly occupied with confusion, contemplation and doubt. I knew I had a lot of other talents, so maybe it was time for me to pursue those interests. Maybe God allowed this to happen because it was time for me to pour more energy into raising my son. Maybe I really was getting too old. Maybe I was too fat. Maybe I wasn't nearly as good as I thought I was. Maybe I was cursed!

"First a painful divorce, now no ESPN contract? No solid job security to raise my son? Holy Cow! I am definitely cursed!" I conjectured with paranoia. "What will I do? Dear God, have mercy on me!" My flair for the pitifully dramatic never had a greater chance to shine than this moment in my life. I sang *"Oh, woe is me"* like it was a Billboard chart topping hit! Perhaps you chuckle, but do you relate?

* * *

ON THE COURT....

Everyone's a Critic

Whether it is the loss of a job, the lack of a promotion or the demise and severance of a relationship, we all at some time experience defeat that leads us to question our worth and value. But before we are defeated, we usually have clues as to why our efforts are not adequately working out. The question is, do we really pay attention and listen to those clues? Do we accept constructive criticism? Are we aware there is a bigger picture beyond our own personal digital image? And most important, are we *coachable*?

If you are truly coachable, you will understand that criticism, no matter how negative it is, can be spun positive if you will it to be. If we are coachable, what we perceive as loss eventually can be used as gain. Being coachable doesn't mean you simply accept constructive criticism. Being coachable means you use it to change and improve.

I've always been amazed how while I was coaching I might say to a player, "Way to score, kid, but you got to do a better job at getting back on defense. We're getting killed on the fast break." What she would hear is, "All you do is shoot, you never play any defense, and you're the reason why we're losing. You are the worst player I have ever seen!"

Find the Truth

Since our earliest comprehension, we have inherently un-derstood the importance of being accepted and valued. We're constantly playing the game of life to win approval. We yearn for our parent's approval. We go to school and begin to desire our teachers to commend us for our smarts or good works. We want our friends to like us. We jump through hoops to capture the eyes then the heart of some really cute guy or the pretty girl. We want praise and promotion from our boss. Then we reverse the cycle of searching for our elders' and peers' approval and revert to wanting our kids to think we're cool.

At our most basic core of existence, what we all want, what we're all playing for, is love and acceptance from one another. That in turns offers us peace and joy. Even if you believe your ultimate gain is money, it isn't long before you discover it can buy you many things, but not real love. Some of the wealthiest people I know are lavished in luxury but lost in the legitimacy of love. "Do you love me for who I really am or what I have?" they wonder. "Would I still be the *Man* if I didn't have the money?" "Is it the person or the possessions you dig?" We fail to see that living our lives with the constant goal to win approval is like playing the basketball game with the goal to win fan support.

The goal should never be as much to be **approved** as it is to be **improved**. When you truly understand the game of basketball as well as life, you'll discover the best players and the real winners play ball because they just love to. They work hard because they want to get better. They accept constructive criticism willfully because they recognize somehow there is a way they can improve from it. If you truly love something (or someone), you are constantly thrilled by the notion you are becoming better in some way to serve that love interest.

If you search the criticism you receive but find nothing valid that you can use to improve, then you can easily discard it as merely someone else's opinion. That opinion is a reflection of who that person is or what they believe and nothing more. You will realize that criticism alone has virtually no direct effect on your outcome. You won't take it personally. It is the sports-minded understanding that fans will either applaud, boo, or both the entire game. The direct effect is nil. An indirect effect is only possible because we choose to allow it to mean something.

When we choose to allow ourselves to hear the fans' cheers, we fill ourselves with the belief that we have support and acceptance.

Yeah! When we choose to hear the heckling and booing, we open up our minds to negativity that is totally counterproductive to what we are trying to do. However, anyone who has ever been in an empty gym or playground blacktop playing a game of hoops with no one on the sidelines realizes they don't need either to actually play the game. They don't need to hear the fans applause to feel good about scoring a basket, making a great assist or winning the game. Similarly, it only takes getting stripped in the backcourt, a string of missed layups, or losing to feel pretty bad about forgetting to bring your A-game. No outside hecklers are necessary.

When you allow yourself to be coachable, you allow yourself a chance to learn, to grow and to change by taking on new perspectives, pushing yourself to limits or following someone else's direction or recommendation. While I've met or known of a few reserved or soft spoken basketball coaches, the majority of the coaches I know are loud, assertive, aggressive and demanding on the court. Most players relate to such behavior with fear, frustration and doubt at first. Once they come to trust and understand that this is just the way their coaches are behaving to get the job done, the screaming, the criticism, the aggression becomes easier to accept and handle, especially if this behavior results in winning.

Change and growth situations in life that arise are a lot like those screaming coaches. They seem demanding and usually aren't particularly sweet and pleasant to deal with. If you can understand that inside every adverse situation exists an opportunity to learn something or to test your strength of character, you will be less likely to let your negative emotions shut down the blessing of growth that lies just beyond your pride, pain or discomfort.

Open Your Mind

I've found that accepting criticism and instruction is often most difficult because you have to deal with the people in authority delivering the comments. Personality clashes can sometimes keep you from finding the value of their instruction. Perhaps you don't like the tone they use, or maybe you just don't trust them. It's not unusual to find that sometimes your coaches have their own personal agendas, vendettas or psychological issues that result in their doling out unfair censure. After all, they are human too, subject to the same emotions and flaws you are, whether they are in charge or not.

You have to have the discernment as well as the peace of spirit to know when there is something valuable you can elicit from a situation and when there is not. You have to always keep the goal in mind of why you are playing the game. Either the instruction you are receiving is going to help you move closer to that goal or it isn't. If it is, are you prepared to make the changes necessary, or will you spend your time evaluating who said it, how it was said, how it should have been handled, etc? If it isn't going to help you, can you readily dismiss it and not let the perceived negativity poison your soul? Best applied, can you live out the doctrine of the Serenity Prayer?

> *"Lord, grant me the serenity to accept the*
> *things I cannot change,*
> *courage to change the things I can and wisdom*
> *to know the difference."*

Consider this little basketball story....

Becky was a shooting guard who transferred to a mid-major university after her freshman year from another mid-major Division-I University. She sat out a required year due to NCAA regulations for collegiate transfers. A brand new coaching staff was hired during her first year of eligibility as a sophomore at the new university. This coaching change for various reasons resulted in a reduction of team members. Thus, Becky was a starter on a team of seven players. The team went 3-25 that year.

By the time her junior year rolled around, Becky, operating on the false security of being good enough to be a starter on a team of seven players the previous season, had the expectation of naturally being a starter yet again. However, this time the roster held 14 players, including six talented, competitive and hungry freshmen, most of whom were also guards and all of whom were hand-picked by the new coach.

Although Becky was a competitor at heart who seemed to love the game (her father was a high school basketball coach), the knock on her game was that she was one-dimensional. She was a very good three-point shooter, arguably the most accurate on the team. However, she had slow feet, was not very athletic overall, and was the team's worst defender. Offensively, her idea of running the offense was to shoot the ball every time she was open, which only proved to be a problem because she *always* thought she was open. All five opponents, the referees, six members of the band and two fans holding popcorn could be defensively surrounding Becky, and she would force up a shot from half court with her eyes closed then look utterly stupefied as to why it didn't go in. She would be equally as perplexed as to why her teammates were furious or why the coach didn't believe in her ability.

Needless to say, Becky was not a starter her junior season. In fact, she was the last player off the bench. I sympathized with how she wrestled with her pride daily under the realization she went from a starter one year to a regular in the DNP (Did Not Play) column game after game the next. She demanded on many occasions to know why she wasn't playing. Unsatisfied with the constructive criticism she would receive from the coaches, she spent many practices pouting, spreading contagious venom to her teammates, her family, and anyone else who would listen that the coaches didn't know what they were doing or just flat out hated her for no reason.

When none of that changed her predicament, she finally attempted to sincerely inquire about what she needed to do to improve and made the effort to work harder in practice. She even came into the gym extra hours to work on her own. The problem with Becky was she was not coachable when it counted. By the time she got over her pity party, all the guests had gone home, especially the one that counted, the head coach.

Becky never seemed to truly *accept the things she could not change*. She often complained that the coach played favoritism toward the players he recruited. If this was indeed true, what could she possibly do to change it? The coach's feelings were his own. Complaining solved nothing. In fact, it only alienated her from the new players and irritated the coach. If she truly felt strongly that this was the reality of her circumstances, she should have focused her energy on having the *courage to change the things she could*.

How much harder would you work if you wanted something badly but knew you were at a disadvantage? Remember, Becky was a transfer student and one of the reasons she transferred was because her previous coach didn't play her due to her lack of defense and speed. Now she was being criticized by her new coach at her new school for the same things.

Becky admitted she did not work hard on these skills in the off season. Improving in these specific areas would have helped her become a better all around player and likely changed the coaches' perception of her usefulness to the team. As far as she knew, the coach may have still preferred the players he recruited, but by listening to what the coach said she needed to do to get better and then actually doing it, Becky likely would have become a visibly better player – something at the very least she could take personal pride in.

She would have been able to position herself for a stronger chance at gaining the playing time she thought she deserved. She also would have helped to raise the level of competition every day in practice, which would only make the rest of the team stronger. Had she been coachable with a "team first" mentality, it would likely have helped her personal circumstances in many ways she never gave enough merit to because she was selfishly focused, prideful and ultimately not coachable.

You're probably asking, "But what if it became visible to everyone on the team and all the coaches that she had greatly improved and was a greater asset to the team, yet the head coach still didn't play her because it was clear he was biased against her?" Wisdom would have to lead her to the understanding that now she has fallen so far behind in the game she may be left with no choice but to put on a full court press.

In this particular situation, however, there was no need to press because Becky was her own worst enemy. If you aren't coachable, you won't ever be able to run an effective press. Pressing requires a lot of risks, tenacity of purpose and strategically defensive intelligence. If you haven't satisfactorily met or exceeded the requirements and expectations of the person in authority, how do you think you will ever begin to assertively or effectively defend your position to anyone?

The first question that will always be asked is, "Did you do what you were asked to do?" The second will be, "Can you prove it?" You must be coachable first! The phrase '*wisdom to know the difference*' in the Serenity Prayer is directly related to asking yourself, "Am I or have I been coachable?"

I made up this little rhyme to help:

> *"Have I respectfully done all I could, the*
> *way authority has said I should,*
> *not just for myself, but for the greater good?"*

Wisdom to know the difference is the most important part of the Serenity Prayer. Becky spent far too much time focusing on the things she could not change and very little time applying herself to the things she could. The world is full of options. The truth is we don't always like those options because they almost always mean working harder, starting over or challenging ourselves beyond our comfort level. So we pour our energies into blaming and focusing on things we cannot change with emotions like anger, frustration and self-pity that do very little to help us play through the fouls.

Being coachable means we are prepared for the mentally tough situations as well as the physical ones. Being coachable means we recognize and respect authority. Being coachable means we have to open our eyes to the fact that what's best for the team has to supersede our own personal agenda. Being coachable means we have to not just accept, but use constructive criticism to improve ourselves as well as our team. Being coachable ain't always easy, folks, but it's absolutely necessary to be a successful player in a game that requires us all to get along and work together for a greater good.

Overcome the Drama Queen Syndrome

It isn't my suggestion that you jump through hoops to change yourself to meet everyone else's approval every time you are corrected or criticized. I am suggesting you at least let down your defenses long enough to try that sneaker on to see if it fits. I also want to make it clear that being coachable never means allowing yourself to be treated unfairly or degraded. But you must be wise enough to understand the difference between being pushed or challenged for growth versus flat out being abused. You must also be honest and wise enough to recognize when you are suffering from a victim's mentality and not a winner's mentality. This is most often characterized by what I call *DQS* (Drama Queen Syndrome).

Drama Queens believe every situation that doesn't work out the way they want it to means they are being used or abused. Being coachable asks you to first do some self-introspection to be sure you are not hindered by DQS. If you don't trust your own self-evaluation, ask friends and family to honestly assess whether they perceive you as someone who consistently struggles with handling authority or accepting constructive criticism.

If you find this is the case, it will always seem like the opponents, the team, the referees, the coaches, the fans, virtually everybody is against you. You will be labeled weak-minded, a hater, a blamer, a pouter, a quitter, a control-freak, a sore loser... the list goes on. Suddenly you will wake up and discover life is not as much a contact sport as it is a miserable solo sport. I promise you, life was never designed to be a solo sport.

I know my fair share about playing solo. After the ESPN pity party, which directly came on the heels of my divorce pity party, I was all partied out and done with working and dealing with people for a while. I even believed my love affair with basketball was over. I just wanted to get away alone and ask God a bunch of "Why me?" questions on a beach somewhere.

So I sold my house, packed up my son and moved down to sunny Florida. My life had been far too cloudy for too long so I thought the change of scenery would do me good. It took me a year and a half to stop being mad at the world.

Meanwhile, my bruised ego and I were becoming best friends. We did everything and went everywhere together! There we sat on the beach when the basketball revelation hit me: I truly had not been coachable throughout the ESPN ordeal. In hindsight, I may not have been very coachable my entire life. I had always just been really good and relatively successful at everything I put my mind to do most of my life. Why be *coached* when I could always just *coast*?

Voted "Most Likely to Succeed" my senior year in high school, I assumed that label to be a prophecy. I was a bit autocratic with perfectionist tendencies, and that always seemed to help propel me into success. I was typically very optimistic that I could do almost anything. What I found out too late was that

I was only coachable when the ball was in my court and I was the star. The day I was told to ride the bench, the minute I was told my game wasn't what it could be, and the second I felt I was fouled, DQS took over!

When the producer at ESPN told me she was looking for A WNBA player or big name coach, I needed to accept immediately I was neither. I could not change my age or my status, nor could I change what she felt she needed to better her team. Like Becky, I was not recruited by the new coach, and I was not her preference. The ESPN "coach" had her own idea of who should be the star of her team. This was her prerogative and it certainly was not something I could change. So why did I let this hurt my feelings or my pride?

When I really gave it a fair look, I realized I had also been offered constructive criticism when I was told my sideline reporting needed work and I could stand to tone down the humor. I believed because the fans would tell me they loved my work and my humor that their praise was more significant than what the coach said she wanted.

My justifications of what the previous ESPN Executive Producer said he liked about me and why I was hired was irrelevant too. He was no longer the coach. She was. The onus was on me to change, not her. Even if she had already made up her mind to replace me, if I were coachable I would have used her criticisms to improve my broadcast skills regardless of the circumstances. I would use the constructive criticism to improve, not to simply be approved.

Finally, I rejected the notion of her "finding some games for me to do" because I was prideful and self-centered. When I was hired to work my very first game at ESPN, I remembered it being the most exciting day of my life. I had waited years for my big break. All I could think about was how excited I was to be a part of the team. I didn't entertain notions of being the star of the team. I was just humbly excited to play my part. I was a true team player.

If this was still my truth, then it should not have affected me so much personally when the person running the team told me she thought it best to go in a direction that didn't include me. If I were coachable, I would have understood that the team's benefit had to always remain my first concern, even if it meant suddenly I had to ride the bench. I would also understand that the coach didn't say, "You are the worst broadcaster I have ever seen; I hate you." But you couldn't tell by the way I acted at the time.

Take It to Heart

When you are not coachable and you struggle with DQS, you will always overdramatize the way you hear unfavorable news. Don't get me wrong... I had a right to feel upset about what was happening to me. I am human with real emotions, and my life was about to endure a major change by her decision. However I do believe I was so upset and angry that I didn't stand a chance to see what I could gain or use out of this adverse situation. I just immediately jumped on the anger, doom and gloom train.

Perhaps going back to doing a few games would have been the perfect opportunity to keep a little income, stay visible in the broadcasting industry, and work on the things she believed I needed to improve upon. I might have still remained a valuable member of the team. After all, I wasn't kicked off the team. I just lost my starting spot so to speak. Nevertheless, I didn't give the thought of sticking around a chance. I decided I didn't like the coach and I quit. Game over.

I share all of this as a point of fact and illustration, not as an admission of regret. Due to my faith, I never allow myself to live with regrets. I believe my life would have been a blessing no matter what my circumstances were with ESPN and the new producer. She may have been the ESPN coach, but the "Ultimate Coach" always sets up another game for me to play, another team for me to contribute to, and more lessons for me to learn and share. I truly believe He just needed me to learn to become more coachable under His direction and get out of my own way. That I did.

It took me to actually become a coach to realize just how un-coachable I had been. After my year and a half of pouting and pondering, I was blessed with an opportunity to begin coaching at the collegiate level and realized that I really was learning the game of hoops from a fresh new perspective. I was using at least one piece of the ESPN producer's constructive criticism by getting recent coaching experience. A few years later when I was asked to join a new television network, I finally found myself benefitting from this piece of her advice.

Coaching definitely helped to make me a more insightful analyst. However, I didn't solely become a better analyst of the game of basketball. I became a better analyst of the game of life. The parallels between the two are indeed astonishing at times. My difficult experiences were never meant to be in vain. They were meant to teach me how to be more coachable so that I might effectively coach others to do the same. Amazing what you can learn and the victories you can celebrate when you allow yourself to be coachable!

WORK THROUGH LIFE'S HURDLES:
Handle the Ball

OFF THE COURT....

In an Instant...

On March 23, 2007 at approximately one o'clock in the morning I unexpectedly came face-to-face with the greatest emotional challenge of my life. The voice on the other end of my cell phone was my father's. Slowly, candidly and concisely the words came from his voice to my rejecting ears.

"Your mom died tonight," he softly lamented.

I was on a bus full of people as our Indiana University Women's Basketball Team was returning from a season-ending defeat in the Women's National Invitational Tournament. A stabbing rush of heat, pain and anxiety filled my chest. I thought surely I would collapse right there in the seat at the front of the bus.

"No!" I screamed so loud that I frightened everyone on board. My father's attempt to comfort me through the phone drifted off like a distant echo. The ensuing details are a painful blur even now as I tremble recalling it all....

Deep inside, amidst the despair, emptiness, stress and grief that trampled up, down and across my entire being, was the reality that somewhere, somehow, I had to find the strength, courage and wisdom to "handle the ball" (if not several of them all at once). I had to address the hectic challenges that face virtually everyone who loses a parent or close loved one and dutifully must orchestrate the necessary death and burial arrangements.

Time allotted for grieving and self-pity seemed all too short. I needed to make immediate arrangements to fly from Indiana to Florida. I needed to quickly pack suitcases. I needed to withdraw some money. I needed to explain grandma's passing to my nine-year old son and give him the standard "try to be strong" instruction I would barely be following myself. He was going to likely miss school for a couple of weeks, so I needed to contact his teacher. I needed to inform my mother's relatives and friends. I needed to plan a funeral, pick out a casket, and decide what clothes Mom would be buried in. I needed to contact a caterer, arrange for limousines and family transportation, and find a host hotel for the slew of relatives and friends that would be flying in from all over the globe. I needed to take care of administrative paperwork involving death certificates, social security, cancellation of credit cards and financial accounts. The to-do list seemed endless!

A million thoughts raced through my head at once. "What was I supposed to do with all of Mom's clothes and personal belongings? How was Dad handling the realization that his wife of 53 years was suddenly gone now? She died right in front of him! How does anybody deal with that?! Will I need to relocate and move back to Florida to take care of him? Where did Mom tell me I would find her Will and all her financial information? She tried to tell me what to do should anything ever happen to her, but I didn't want to listen. That was just far too sad and morbid to think about, and Mom was going to live forever, anyway. She just had too much spunk and spirit to die of a heart attack at 75! Is she in Heaven now? Can she see me? Can she hear me? Does she know how very confused, weak and insane I feel at this moment talking to myself, spinning in circles, crying like a two-year-old?"

I had lots of questions and seemingly no answers.

Despite the gracious and loving concern of my friends, I never felt more alone and lost than at that time in my life. It was much like that dreadful feeling that would overcome me when an important basketball game was on the line and I was the point-guard trying to dribble the ball up the court against a full court press. I couldn't find anyone open to pass the ball to. I had no time outs. Everyone was anxiously watching me, wondering what I would do under such extreme pressure, praying for the best but fully expecting me to lose it against such challenging odds.

No matter what anyone said or did, nothing was going to change the fact that my mother, the matriarch, was now gone. With a 79-year-old father and a brother who had spent the previous three years of his life incarcerated, ultimately the bulk of the responsibility of keeping affairs in order and the family together would be mine. That reality, combined with a crippling grief I had never before experienced, sent my heart racing and my head spinning at unprecedented speeds.

"How am I supposed to **handle** all of this?" I screamed to the Heavens, not sure if anyone would actually answer. Oddly enough, my answer came.

"Remember What's Most Important...."

Those words flashed across my mind like a dancing ghost of light. It was the title of a wall scroll my mother had given to me as a gift just two weeks earlier following a 15-hour road trip we made from Bloomington, Indiana to Jacksonville, Florida. It was a gift I received from her the last day I saw her alive.

She came into the guest room of her home where I was sleeping, and pulled the scroll out from behind her back saying, "I picked this up for you. I thought the words were perfect."

"Mom, please tell me you didn't get this at that truck stop!" I giggled back.

We chuckled because Mom was a shopaholic and was always buying little trinkets and tidbits, sometimes for no other reason than because it was a bargain or on sale. I'm just like her. This time her choice selection definitely proved to have a good, perhaps even prophetic reason.

She confirmed that she had picked it up from a truck stop in Georgia. I read it out loud with her standing there in front of me. I could still vividly see her image and that moment on this dark night of questions and despair. Suddenly those words held great value and significance. Suddenly instead of questions, I was starting to get my answers:

"Remember What's Most Important"
by Vickie M. Worsham

It's not having everything go right;
It's facing whatever goes wrong.
It's not being without fear;
It's having the determination to go in spite of it.
It's not where you stand,
but the direction you're going in.
It's more than never having bad moments;
It's knowing you are bigger than the moment.
It's believing you have already been given
everything you need to handle life.
It's not being able to rid the world of its injustices;
It's being able to rise above them.
It's the belief in your heart that there will be

more good than bad in the world.
Remember to live just this one day
and not add tomorrow's trouble to today's load.
Remember that every day ends and brings
a new tomorrow full of exciting new things.
Love what you do, do the best you can,
and always remember how much you are loved.

With that memory firmly in my mind, I walked to my bedroom where I had hung the scroll. Almost as if possessed, I stood there reading it over and over again until I gained a sense of clarity. More than anything, the words *"It's believing you have already been given everything you need to handle life"* stood out from all the rest. It played over and over again in my head.

My mother, my most trusted friend, my favorite laughing, shopping and gossiping buddy, was gone. As for me, I was left to *handle* life. I was getting a crash-course lesson that a huge part of handling life was handling death. The pain, the grief, the mourning, the loneliness and the confusion are all part of the process of accepting mortality, others' as well as the inevitable reality of our own.

After a week or so, the funeral plans were completed, the administrative processes were started, the grieving relatives and loved ones who had come to comfort and pay their respects were now back home. Somehow, I got through it all.

Admittedly, though, the emotional pain and loss was far from gone. In many ways, it was just beginning. Yet all the seemingly hundreds of things I once fretted over getting done got done, and they were handled relatively quickly, even if numbly. Through faith, diligence and persistence, I realized that even in the face of a loved one's death, somehow we are granted the fortitude to bounce back. We don't always know how exactly, but we seem to innately respond when the ball is in our court and we realize we have to handle it the best way we know how. We do what we need to do.

Great appreciation is due to the love and compassion of comforting family and friends who help us get through it. But given the many lonely moments and internal struggles we face independent of all others, God's faithful gifts of self-reliance, strength and coping deserves high praise. While some people do fumble and drop the ball or choose not to handle it at all, most people do keep on dribbling and advancing toward the goal of living rather than dying. Despite our troubles, our grief and our sadness, we truly do discover we have already been given everything we need to handle life. We choose life because life somehow chooses us. Bit by bit, step by step, we handle that rock and we go on.

Nothing will ever replace the love I have for my mother, and I will always remember the special bond we shared. Over time in dealing with her loss I have found it quite remarkable how almost in spite of myself I managed to bounce back. A lot of that has to do with first choosing to *"remember what's most important."*

Life is important and ever so precious. I've learned that nothing seems to make that more clear than the moment we realize life is no more for someone we dearly love.

***

ON THE COURT....

Stay in Control

For most of us, the first time we held a basketball in our hands, we pounded it down to the floor and attempted to dribble it. Our little child hands and minds were fascinated at how it came back up to us whenever we pushed it down. I remember attempting to control the ball by swatting wildly at it with an open hand. As I matured I learned that there was a technique, a more controlled rhythm to dribbling the basketball. By the time I became an actual basketball player, I learned dribbling is not merely about technique; it is about purpose. It is about relatively small but consistent movements intended to advance a player (as well as a team) toward a goal or a better position.

The most powerful player in the game is the one with possession of the basketball, because he or she is most in control at any given moment to score. It's also important to remember that the person in possession of the basketball, or the "ball handler," is not always in the best position to score. The basket may be too far away to take a reasonable shot or the person may be closely guarded or defended in a manner that would make scoring extremely difficult.

There is a concept in the game of hoops known as the "triple threat," meaning that the person with the ball always has three options: shoot, pass or dribble. Clearly, when a player is not in the best position to score, he or she must exercise one of the other two options, to pass or to dribble. Passing is usually thought of as the next best and most unselfish option. After all, passing is the fundamental networking function of team play. But what happens when there isn't a teammate perceivably open enough to pass the ball to? Suddenly, dribbling is the best, if not the only option available, and the ability to dribble and handle that ball under pressure is most critical.

Of the three triple threat options, dribbling is the only one that keeps the ball in a player's complete control. Dribbling is the aspect of handling the ball with little, deliberate movements that keeps the game moving. It is the "in the meantime" option we must execute until we figure out how to get into better position to score.

In life, the consistent, rhythmic little things we do are our methods of dribbling or handling the ball. It's been said that it's the little things in life that matter most. Dribbling is one of those little things. When giving instruction at camps and clinics, I often like to dedicate entire segments to ball handling drills. After all, good coaches teach the fundamentals of protecting the basketball while staying centered and balanced. Staying centered and balanced is an awesome life strategy or technique in the face of adversity as well.

After learning the fundamentals of staying centered and balanced, you also learn additional ball handling skills, like how to change your pace or direction while keeping your head up and advancing toward the goal. The most complete ball players are the ones who master handling the ball, whether on the court or off of it.

Push Forward

You are the ball handler in your game of life and will always have decisions to make. Some decisions you'll need to make quickly, in snap judgment or even on impulse in response to the flow of the game. Other times you will find yourself in the backcourt, slowly advancing the ball up court as you contemplate what play your life should be running next, who to pass to if needed, and how to get to the goal. Most important, you have to understand that when the ball is in your hands, you and you alone are in control. You have to confidently find your rhythm, dribble that ball and advance the best way you know how.

Yes. At times it may seem easier to just hold the ball and do nothing. But just like in the game of basketball, you can only stop and do nothing for so long. If you don't make a move, you will either be whistled for a violation for delaying the flow of the game, or you will find yourself surrounded and trapped by the opposition. When you do nothing, you relinquish your power, turn over the ball, and find yourself suddenly in defensive mode, fighting for a chance to get the ball back. The game of life like basketball is one that is meant to keep moving while doing the little things necessary to stay in control.

I admit that when I first received news that my mother died, I felt far from being in control and I didn't feel like I could move at all. I didn't feel like I would ever want to move again, really. The point is, however, I *had* to. The rules were clear: I had to handle the ball, and I had a limited amount of time where I could hold onto it and do nothing.

Regardless of my grief or pain, plans had to be made. Things had to get done. Mom had passed, but I was still part of the living team, and hence, the game had to go on. It would go on with me in control or without. The choice was mine. But undoubtedly, the game would go on.

In dealing with the loss of my mother, I had to understand first what the goal was and second, *where* the goal was. I was so lost and turned around for a moment that I understood neither.

I decided the goal, as best as I could perceive it, was a combination of finding acceptance, sanity, peace, coping and eventually even feeling joy again. I also decided that goal was likely far away. It seemed like the basketball court in my game of life had lengthened far past the regulation 94-feet. It felt more like 1,094-feet. Feeling this far from the goal would require some serious ball handling on my part!

I was the point guard in this very trying situation. I was in charge of not just me, but also in charge of helping my team (my family) get through this very trying time. A lot of things needed to get done at a time when I least felt like doing anything. I realized nothing could or would get done all at once. I had to get myself under control and try to complete one small task at a time.

In truly difficult times, as in dealing with loss, it is the persistent, consistent and small steps combined with the deliberate pounding our way up and down, around and through that we find our way. Remember, a good ball handler demonstrates the ability to keep his or her head up while staying low to the ground, centered, focused and balanced through the pressure and chaos as he or she finds a way to move ahead. A good ball handler understands that quitting, holding the ball too long or throwing the thing away are not favorable options. We may feel the most vulnerable when the ball is in our hands and our triple threat options have been reduced to the autocracy of the dribble. It is then, however, that we must remember we are actually the most powerful.

If you have ever experienced great loss but didn't quit even though you may have quivered, then you have learned the great lesson of handling the ball. The game doesn't stop just because you are far from the goal. The game expects and requires you to dribble your way into position to have a chance at scoring again.

To date, you no doubt have had countless obstacles and adversity, yet here you stand with most of them behind you. The adversities and obstacles you have been faced with throughout life are truly just ball handling drills teaching you the patience, the rhythm and the step-by-step persistence required to constantly get out of the backcourt and into the front court of your life where you can score.

Constantly remember what's most important here – that you've already been given everything you need to handle life. You just need to decide that you want to handle it and be prepared to bounce back...over and over and over again. We all experience loss and have to somehow deal with the grief, the pain, the uncertainty and the challenges that inevitably accompany it. There is truly no way to avoid it just as there is no way to play a basketball game without dribbling the ball.

"*It's just the way the ball bounces.*" So handle it....and you'll likely prove to be a better player than you ever thought you could be.

BE THERE FOR OTHERS:
Make the Assist

OFF THE COURT....

An Unlikely Soul Mate

Pat had five teeth. I counted them. I've always been fixated by people's mouths.

I'm a big smile person by nature. I've always believed nice lips and pretty teeth are what make a great smile. Where many people are attracted to eyes, I see the mouth first. So I was immediately certain Pat had only five teeth. All of them were brown and decayed, randomly spaced apart inside a mouth that reeked of hygienic neglect and showed obvious signs of malnourishment.

Pat was a seventy-something homeless woman I found nestled beneath old clothing and blankets on Jacksonville Beach one cold November morning. For reasons I cannot explain outside of God's gentle urging to reveal my sense of humanity and decency, I stopped to ask her if I could buy her a cup of coffee.

"Oh, that would be wonderful," she said. That's when she smiled at me revealing those five meager teeth. Although there was nothing even remotely attractive about this woman by conventional shallow standards, I felt uncontrollably drawn in and bonded.

"What's your name?" I asked.

"Pat. My name is Pat," she responded as she looked up at me through a pair of white fashion-wear sunglasses with rhinestones in the corners of the frame. I immediately decided she had found them lying on the beach somewhere, as it was easy to deduce everything she possessed had to be scraps or remnants of someone else's forgetfulness or undesirability.

Sadly, I imagined Pat likely felt she too was a remnant of society's forgetfulness or undesirability. She was one of the many homeless and hungry transients who called the Jacksonville Beach shores home.

On her head was a blue, gray and brown checked pair of men's boxers that she adorned like a floppy hat. A lime green, partially torn, small blanket was draped around her neck like a winter scarf. She wore a black sweatshirt underneath a larger red, lintball covered sweatshirt on her torso, both of which were turned inside out so that the inner stitching and tags showed. She had a flower print sheet tied around her waist to make a skirt.

As I was walking along the beach, it was the sheet that caught my attention. It was flapping in the wind as Pat was on her knees adjusting her belongings so that she could make herself a comfortable place to rest. The opening in that wrap-around sheet revealed her light brown, wrinkled backside, naked and free for all eyes to see! I couldn't help but chuckle. Next thing I knew, I was standing next to her asking if I could help.

It was the coldest morning of the season. Typically Jacksonville doesn't experience a severe fall or winter. Lows may reach the mid 30s to low 40s on an average night, giving way to 65 to 75-degree days this time of year.

The night before, however, it dropped down to 27-degrees. Now, shortly after sunrise, it still felt every bit as cold. The day's high was only expected to be a chilly 51. Despite the cold, I was having one of those mornings where I was feeling down and I needed a chance to get away and think. Walking the beach always helps me do this. I love the beach, even when it's chilly. But I couldn't imagine ever having to sleep in the natural elements of the sand, wind, water and cold. Pat could. Pat did regularly, and I was saddened by that reality, feeling almost ashamed of my own modest prosperity.

I had on a thick, hooded Nike fleece sweat suit. Nike! Pat wore a no-name sheet and torn sweatshirts someone else had thrown in the trash. She had neither shoes nor socks and her feet looked badly worn and blistered. I had on Nike running shoes and socks that snugly comforted and cushioned my toes as they paced my feet and body's movement to the sounds downloaded into my 80GB iPod Classic. Pat didn't have music, except the melody inside her own soul that she consolably hummed aloud. I smelled of a fresh morning shower, Secret deodorant and a Bath and Body Works fragrance. Pat emitted a sour scent of stale urine and sea water.

"Pat, I'm Vera. Nice to meet you," I melodically chimed out. "You must be cold, Sweetie."

"It's a little cold, but I'm okay," Pat answered as she continued to adjust her blanket and sheets around her lap and shoulders. Pat had a bit of a lisp, courtesy of her missing teeth.

"It may take me a while to walk down to the McDonald's, but I'll be right back with some coffee to warm you up," I continued.

"I'll be right here, and thank you so much," Pat replied.

A Desire to Help

I felt a surge of emotion as I walked away – part pity of her circumstances; part anxiety over whether I remembered to bring some money to the beach; part excitement and sense of humanitarian purpose; part disgust that society didn't do more to help;

and part thankfulness to God for my own blessings, which seemed to radiate more apparent than ever at this moment. But I was also thankful for the blessing of compassion and humility I was feeling right then that led me to listen to the little voice inside me that whispered, "Here's your chance to make an assist."

When I arrived at my car I was relieved to find that this was one of those few times I actually had a little cash in my purse. I also had my ATM card. Suddenly a cup of coffee alone wasn't good enough for my new friend Pat. Surely coffee would warm her up, but she had to be so very hungry. Greater, she had to be so very cold.

Before I walked over to the McDonald's, I made a decision to scamper over to the Walgreens just a couple of blocks away. Inside I found a pink sweatshirt and stood for several minutes trying to locate the matching pink bottoms. After pulling through all the colors and sizes, I had to settle on a beige pair of bottoms. They were the only "feminine" looking sweats among the crop of mismatched blacks, blues and olive greens in the batch.

I remember talking to myself out loud saying, "What does Pat care if they match or what color they are? She'll just be happy to have some warm clothes." But I decided that maybe just a little added touch of feminine or fashionable flair might make her feel more like a woman of style than a woman of stigma, even if only for a moment.

That thought led me to the soaps and lotions aisle. How nice would it be to take a bath with sweet smelling soap and apply some luxurious lotion to her wind and sun chafed skin for a change? I know it seemed silly for a woman who likely had to bathe in the ocean, but I decided even vapors of the salty and fishy Atlantic could be enhanced with some Pomegranate-scented body wash, perfume, lotion and powder on a woman's skin. Plus the neat and cute little carrying bag might prove helpful in the future.

I started to pick up some toothpaste and a toothbrush but changed my mind once I reasoned Pat's five teeth were long past the benefits of Crest or Colgate. I then ventured over into the snack aisle. I wanted to get her something healthy, so I grabbed a box of granola bars. It then occurred to me that as good as I thought they would taste, trying to chew them would probably seem almost like cruelty to Pat. So I got the softer chewy granola instead.

As I continued to look for more things to give, I realized that Pat had to carry everything she had everywhere she went. These items, as helpful as they might prove to be, would become burdensome if she had to lug them around with all the rest of her stuff. So my last item was a large tote bag that she could sling over her shoulder and go.

Once out of my Walgreens shopping spree, I finally headed over to the McDonald's. I ordered the Egg McMuffin combo meal. I wasn't sure what Pat might be allergic to or what she would or wouldn't eat. I didn't want my efforts to help end up making her sick. I prayed the McMuffin and hash browns would be safe.

To my surprise, this particular McDonald's didn't allow customers to fix their own coffee. You had to request exactly how much cream and sugar you wanted and allow them to prepare it behind the counter. I forgot to ask Pat how she liked her coffee, but I figured she wouldn't like it black. I never could get my mind wrapped around that whole black coffee thing. Yuck! Only a very specialized palate could actually handle it that way.

Since I deeply believed Pat and I were temporary soul mates, I ordered her coffee the way I liked it: medium cream and lots of sweetener. I grabbed napkins and Pat's bagged order and placed them inside the tote bag with the Walgreens goodies. Then I picked up the pre-made coffee and headed out the door back down the beach. I was really excited, like the way I feel when someone is about to open the gift I wrapped for them on their birthday, hoping they will like it or need it and praying it is an adequate expression of my love.

Simple Blessings

I've always found it funny how therapeutic it is to do something helpful, thoughtful or meaningful to assist someone else. We all have the capacity to become very self-absorbed at times. Our troubles seem to magnify because we place ourselves in higher importance than we really should, making our problems seem bigger than they really are.

Whatever was heavy on my mind when I came to the beach had dissipated now. All I thought about and all I wanted to do was something really nice for Pat at this moment. I tried to act cool, because that's just how I roll, you know. But inside I was almost giddy. I have always said if I ever came into a lot of money, I would do something very special for the hungry and homeless. That would be my concentrated area of philanthropy. What I realized at this moment as Pat reached up to take her coffee is that we all have the ability to be philanthropists, even if only on a small scale, every day. Money doesn't have as much to do with it as we sometimes think.

"I picked up a few things for you while I was gone, Pat. I thought maybe you could use them. I hope you can," I humbly offered.

Just then I also extended my hand with some folded cash and told her to use it for bus fare or another meal or two if she wanted. She gladly accepted. She tucked it away and then began to pull the gifts out her tote bag. It was an absolutely amazing feeling to watch Pat open up her tote bag to find her breakfast and her gifts. She reminded me of a little child at Christmas wondering what special surprises Santa had in store for her.

"Oh, what a blessing! Will you look at this?" she squealed. Over and over again she repeated what a blessing everything was and how God is good. She loved the body wash gift set and said she bet it would sure feel good against her skin when she washes up in the ocean.

I was so happy because I didn't want to offend her. In truth, Pat smelled really bad, but I didn't want her to know I was thinking it. That would surely have ruined my good intentions and make her feel ashamed. But it all worked out just fine.

Pat was so genuinely grateful and happy for everything. What I felt inside was almost angelic. I wasn't looking for permission or praise. I just saw a need to help and I was determined to do so the best I knew how. So many times I have walked past beggars and transients unsure of whether I should toss them a few dollars, buy them a meal, or just get away quickly before I got mauled or robbed. It's unfortunate, but there are con artists and scams everywhere. Even when you want to do the right thing, it could prove to be the wrong thing just by the nature of your ignorance of lurking evil.

There are other times, however, that something inside me has said, "Stop and try to help." I can't fully explain it; I just know I have to listen and follow that voice. I think we all get that voice. I'm just not sure we all are obedient to it. It's too bad because the rewards are usually great on both the giving and receiving end. As my mother always used to say, "There by the grace of God go I." Pat could be me and I could be Pat. Given that thought, how could I *not* help?

I kneeled down in front of Pat as she began a conversation that would last well over forty minutes. She sipped her coffee and took a bite of her McMuffin. Mostly, she just talked and talked. Pat had a lot to say and a lot of stories to tell. A storyteller myself at heart, I was fully engaged.

She told me how she had been protecting another homeless woman's property wrapped up in a brown comforter. The police had come to take her friend to jail, and Pat had promised she would keep the woman's things until she returned.

Other transients had tried to steal the woman's things while Pat was sleeping and a few offered her money to sell various items to them.

Pat said it had been rough on her, but she was determined to keep her promise. She had recently received word that the woman would be getting out of jail in five days. She said she was looking forward to having her friend back, but probably more happy to not have to carry all her junk around anymore. It was killing her back!

Pat had a sense of humor! Maybe we really were temporary soul mates.

Living on Hope

I didn't want to pry, but I had to know how Pat got into her homeless predicament. She shared with me that she had five children and she had been staying with the oldest boy, Tyrone, but he had ten kids himself. It got to be that there was just no room for her. She had a daughter who lived here but she was always in and out of trouble. She told me she had another daughter who she believed was now working at a local Winn Dixie but she didn't know which one. She'd tried to locate her to no avail. Another son was staying with a "big old fat woman" who didn't like Pat because she kept throwing their drugs away.

"The woman and my son was always leaving that damn mess around the house out in the open, and the woman got a young daughter, you know? I used to watch after her. I didn't want her to get into it. I couldn't believe they'd do that in front of that baby and all. So whenever I'd see it, I'd flush it down the toilet. That woman got so mad at me! Ooh, baby, you just don't know! I ain't never seen nobody mad like that big old fat woman! Tyrone, he took her side and put me out. So I had to get outta there."

Pat was an animated storyteller. For a moment her accounts

seemed fictional, even funny. When the reality hit me that they were autobiographical, I felt like I might cry. Having spent over a year dealing with the loss of my own mother, I couldn't imagine how any child, let alone five of them, would let the woman that brought them life live homeless and hungry in the cold. Maybe Pat wasn't a saint, but I just couldn't imagine all of her children choosing to allow her to suffer this fate.

There was no way for me to know the whole truth of how Pat ended up on the beaches of Jacksonville. I only got to hear Pat's side of the story. It was a sad story indeed. I doubted that a cup of coffee and a few Walgreens gifts would do very much to change that story. Yet as I was getting up to leave, I noticed there was a book lying beside Pat on the ground. It had a Biblical or spiritual title that I cannot recall, but I remember the words "Living" and "Hope" on the cover. I surmised that the only way Pat made her living from day to day was with a whole lot of hope: hope for reuniting with her children; hope for adequate shelter and clothing; hope that she might eat; hope for companionship; hope for a simple cup of coffee and someone to talk to, even if just for a little while.

The coffee, the breakfast and the gifts were nice gestures, yet I realized it was the intangible of hope that mattered most. There's tremendous power in caring and having a sincere desire to help. It's a blessing just to be able to help, to let another know he or she is not totally alone, but that he or she has a teammate, even if only a temporary one in a random pick-up game.

The best players find purpose and joy in wanting to make assists so that another might score. Even if the recipient doesn't score right away, it's in knowing someone actually passed the ball and offered a chance to score that sometimes matters. I more clearly understand now that in this life when we feel there is little we can do for others, we can always pass them a dish of compassion and hope. Often, that is just enough to make them want to keep on playing and go on living this game of life. What you receive in return is as priceless as Pat's five-toothed grin and the final "God Bless You" she extended as I turned to leave the beach that day.

By the way, I now know that nice lips and pretty teeth don't make half as great a smile as the smile that comes from having a humble and encouraged heart and a genuinely grateful soul. Pat taught me that.

* * *

ON THE COURT....

The Consummate Helper

It's NBA basketball trivia time! Ready? Who is the NBA's All-Time career assists leader? If you screamed out Michael Jordan (always the most popular guess for any kind of NBA trivia), you are wrong – way wrong. That title belongs to John Stockton who played 19 seasons with the Utah Jazz, where he amassed an amazing 15,806 assists.

To give you some idea of how amazing and presumably untouchable this record is, the second place career assists holder is Mark Jackson with 10,334, followed by the highly celebrated Magic Johnson who tallied 10,141. John Stockton sits more than 5,000 assists ahead of some of the greatest professional basketball players in the world, with a record most experts predict is not likely to ever be broken. In the NBA he will be immortalized not for being a great scorer, but for being the greatest "helper."

John Stockton's teammate of 18 seasons, Karl Malone, said it best, "There absolutely, positively, will never ever be another John Stockton – ever." (Hoopedia.nba.com) Malone, nicknamed "The Mailman," should know because he sits second in the NBA record books with 36,928 career points behind Kareem Abdul-Jabbar. It was John Stockton that helped Malone get there with plenty of little assisted packages for The Mailman to deliver.

Historically, an assist was considered to be the pass that immediately preceded a player scoring a basket without the scorer's use of a dribble. The "assistor" was the person who made the pass to his scoring teammate, and therefore was credited with the assist.

As the rules changed over the years, it was decided the assist should be more than a routine pass that precedes a scored basket. It was also reasoned that the philosophical emphasis of the assist should be placed on whether the passer had intentions as well as the savvy to directly lead a teammate to score the basket. How the scorer maneuvered or whether the scorer dribbled was not nearly as important as the pass itself arriving into the player's hands when he or she was in a positional advantage or open to score. It is now understood that the value of the assist lies in a player recognizing a teammate with a definitive opportunity to score and delivering the ball in a timely and direct manner so that he or she can.

Life's assists are so significantly parallel. The value of our helping, whether it is monetarily, materially, emotionally or even spiritually, lies in realizing our fellow life-teammates are either in need or in a current opportune position to "score," and then timely and directly helping them to do this. Just as the basketball rule makers discovered, the intent to make the assist matters.

Certainly our everyday routine passes to one another are important because they are the functional networking in our game of life. However, what makes truly helping or assisting one another so special is when we 1.) Identify a need or opportunity; 2.) Consciously desire to help; 3.) Recognize the means in which we can help; and then, 4.) *"Share the wealth, be the helper, feed the post, dish the rock, or drop that dime, baby!"* as we flowery and verbose commentator-types love to say.

The beauty of the assist is truly the humility of it all. I doubt John Stockton ever sat back and counted every pass he made to a teammate who scored. His smooth playmaking ability was phenomenal and seemed to be unconsciously inherent. Stockton had a knack for just knowing when his teammates were in or about to be in a great position to score.

Old video footage demonstrates times when Karl Malone was in the post trying to get position against a defender and before he knew it, the ball was in his hands, leading him to the open side of the basket away from the defense. It was pure poetry in motion to watch Stockton handle the point and dish out one assist after another to lead his team to victory. In 19 years, however, even his best artistry never amounted in an NBA championship for John Stockton and the Utah Jazz. This fact never took away from Utah always being recognized as a formidable title contender under Stockton's leadership...nor did it outshine Stockton's place in history as the greatest NBA "helper" of all time.

What John Stockton probably figured out early on is that every time he made a great pass to a teammate who was in good position didn't necessarily mean a basket would be scored. However, he did know that his responsibility was to get the ball into the open man's hands. Many times he did just that and his teammate still missed the ensuing shot. That never deterred Stockton from continuing to dish the rock, nor did that ever stop the subsequent high fives or finger points from his appreciative teammates.

The subsequent "Oohs" and "Ahs" and applause from the crowd were further recognition and admiration for Stockton having the presence of mind to see the opportunity and at the very least deliver the "hope" to score and to win. That hope translated into inspired teammates to work harder at their individual performances while elevating Stockton to a career mark and NBA best 15,806 assists in his.

Pass the Ball

When you reach out to help someone out of the pure motives of sincerity in your heart, you are placing the ball in the open man's hands. Your teammate shouldn't always have to call out, "Hey, pass the ball to me," for you to recognize your pass might put them in a position to score. You should consciously know it.

If you are incapable of passing the ball because of the challenges of your own opposition at the time, that's one thing. However, if you refuse to pass the ball because you are selfish or would rather overlook a teammate, for whatever reason, when they are most in need of a chance to score, that's inexcusable. Understand that it is not your position to become an enabler. You're being asked to make the pass so your teammate can score. You're not supposed to get into his position and actually take the shot for him. That's not how the game is supposed to be played. But much like a park pick-up game, we sometimes ball hog and make up the rules as we go along with little to no chance of feeling unified as a team when the game is through.

You must also understand that much like John Stockton, you will reap the rewards even if your teammate misses a wide open shot after you passed the ball. Remember, the value of the assist lies in the intention and the diligence to make the pass, not how the shot is or is not scored after it. For without the intention of the assist, there would be no line of hope to unite one teammate to another to score in the first place.

It is in the passing to one another, especially when we are in the best position to score, that motivates and elevates us to want to not just play the game, but to play the game with togetherness in mind – the way our "Ultimate Coach and Rule Maker" intended. God has always intended for us to be teammates and it is the humility of the assist that joyfully unites us.

Here's a final playmaking note to consider: The assist maker dropping dimes may seem small in comparison to the fact the scorers seem to get the big bucks, and seemingly all the attention and glory. Helping someone else at times may mean a relative sacrifice of your own goals, needs, accomplishments or accolades. That's where the true humility of assisting reveres at its greatest.

The sacrifice is relative, however, because it depends on how you look at the big picture. The big picture is the one that's *not* all about you – it's not the self-centered, little smiling headshot in your favorite scrapbook. It is about contributing to the greater whole so that not one, but all might win.

Realize that giving, helping or assisting doesn't have to equate to playing the role of sacrificial lamb or martyr because selflessness is actually more self serving than we realize. When we give we are always receiving something intrinsically good in return. In essence, in the big picture, making an assist is not really much of a sacrifice at all. It depends on you and where your head and heart are.

It is no wonder the rule makers were slow to acknowledge the specifics for assists record keeping. I think it was always just understood that we are supposed to help one another. The game of basketball cannot and will not function properly if teammates don't pass to one another...and neither will the game of life.

If suddenly there was excessive exuberance and overabundance of recognition for just passing the ball with no intention of actually scoring the thing, everybody would just want to be a great passer. What kind of game would that be? The assist should not outshine the scoring of the basket, because scoring is the goal. Winning is the goal. But the assist should also never be taken for granted, for without it we do not play as a team, but rather as a bunch of individuals fending for self, caring little about anything else. What kind of game would that be? Unfortunately, too many of us are playing this game right now.

As a child I first learned to play basketball by myself, so I got to call the shots. Next thing I knew I had to actually share! I had to pass the ball when I was becoming so good at dribbling and shooting it alone. Yet I, like most players, soon learned basketball is far more enjoyable when you play with others.

While we still work, practice and play to improve our individual performances, we do this ultimately to become better producers within and for the team. We are fully expected to take the shots available to us, but we are also expected to share the rock so others might score as well. The game is about balance. No one person should do all the scoring and no one person should do all of the assisting, but we discover our gifts along the way and we maximize whatever our talents are for the good of the team. Isn't that what the games of hoops and life are really about?

Here's a final piece of trivia: In addition to John Stockton's all time career assist record, he also was a great scorer. Stockton holds a career shooting percentage of .515, which is considered rare excellence for a point guard, not to mention he still ranks in the top 30 of All Time Scorers in the NBA. He also led the league in steals twice and retired as the All-Time Steals leader.

Although he was proven to be a very capable scorer and multi-talented on the hardwood, it was in making the assist to his teammates so that they could be great and his team could be greater that he is most celebrated. He was always making the little plays that helped to get his teammates in the game and made them better in so many ways. He understood the team picture and rarely settled for just the headshot.

Critics may whisper that Stockton, Malone and the Jazz still never won an NBA Championship in all those years. But what they fail to realize is that when your legacy lives on as being a team contributor and being the consummate "helper" (especially when you are indisputably the best in the world), you don't need to win a championship to be considered a **Champion**.

TRY, TRY AGAIN:
Rebound Relentlessly

An Unsung Accolade

I'm divorced and I'm a single mom. It took me a long time to be able to say that completely and honestly without feeling ashamed. When it first became apparent to me that I had joined this increasingly alarming American statistic, I found no strength in the numbers, no company in the misery. I felt alone, defeated and lost.

Wasn't I voted "Most Likely to Succeed" by my senior class at Friendly High School in Fort Washington, Maryland in the 80s? Wasn't I the South Carolina's Broadcasting Association's "Personality of the Year" in the 90s? Wasn't I just voted into the Syracuse University Hall of Fame in 2002?

I replayed every decade of my life, searching every accolade or honor, trying to find some semblance of significance or value in being "me." I could find none. All I could find was hurt and embarrassment, because I had recently faced "D-day." Instead of the cozy, over-romanticized, married life I had always dreamed of, I was now forced to check the "Divorced" box on all my surveys and applications for probably the rest of my life, which to me screamed out to anyone reading it that I was a relationship LOSER!

Of all the adversity I had ever faced to this point in my life, my separation and subsequent divorce from Stephen was by far the most embarrassing, hurtful and unbearable. There is no scientific or medical apparatus that can adequately measure, nor words to powerfully express the depths of the pain you experience when you feel betrayed by the one you love. At times I've struggled to write this book, particularly this chapter, because I couldn't figure out how to tell my truth without re-living the painful memories, without vilifying Stephen, and without hearing the words "Relationship Loser" echo at nauseam in my head.

What has finally come to my rescue is the anecdote of the "rebound." If there is a Hall of Fame Award available for a woman who has learned the art of rebounding, I humbly but confidently nominate myself. I spent roughly seven long years as the "Rebounding Queen." It wasn't a title I necessarily relished, but it definitely beat "Loser" by a long shot.

From the Heights of Passion to Rock Bottom

Stephen and I first met in 1984 when I was a freshman and he was a sophomore at Syracuse University. He had a crush on my roommate, so he was always hanging around our dorm. His crush never amounted to anything serious. In fact, serious wasn't part of the plan. Stephen liked to have fun, and so did I. He was good looking and a barrel of laughs. He was easy to get along with and became popular in our circles as the Dee-jay at all the cool parties and nightspots on campus. Everyone seemed to know "DJ Squid."

He also loved basketball and we always seemed to run into each other at pick-up games at one of the local parks in the summertime. We immediately knew we shared a passion for music, hoops and laughter. We cultivated a casual friendship built around these commonalities.

In 1990, a couple of years after I graduated from Syracuse, Stephen and I began working together at a local radio station. During that time we grew closer and eventually embarked upon a serious relationship. We had more emotional ups and downs than either one of us cared to imagine possible, and yet every break up somehow led us right back into each other's arms, laughing and confessing our undying love to each other once again.

We creatively weaved our love affair into our morning radio show, and the Syracuse listening audience ate our silly soap-opera skits up for more than two years. Our "Sweet V and DJ Squid in the Mornings" show was quite the hit on the small but legendary AM1490-WOLF radio station. I could never imagine our real life would actually grow into a soap opera of epic proportions and change our lives forever.

After six years of mostly on again, but occasionally off again dating, Stephen finally proposed. I was 29 years old and singing that, "Holy Cow, I'm almost 30 and still not married" song almost daily. Stephen was still very financially and emotionally unsure of himself and his maturity. I was overly ambitious and ready to take on the world, fearing that as soon as 30 would hit, my professional life would be over and I would be confined to a walker while taking my daily Geritol supplements and sipping Ensure shakes through a straw.

I had been the maid of honor in two best friend's weddings, attended at least three more in the past year, and just received an invitation from a younger cousin for his wedding engagement. I was outdone. I was sure I had just wasted six good years of my life hoping Stephen would ride in on his courageous steed and rescue me from falling into the 30-year-old single woman abyss. I wasted no time in letting him know I felt his non-commitment meant I was good enough to be his playmate, but not good enough to be his soul mate. I wanted out.

Two weeks later, in what my cousin and a couple of friends said was a risky fit of desperation, Stephen proposed. I was back to being happy and in love with him all over again. My mother, who like most mothers took it upon herself to regularly ask "when are you going to finally settle down and get married?"(as if she were receiving a substantial commission check for each inquiry), was ecstatic when I told her the news. She really liked Stephen, but being the sharp and instinctive type questioned whether we might have what it took to be in it for the long haul. (She would be the one who knew what it takes. At the time of her passing my mother and father had been married 53 years.) Still, those instincts and fears never kept her from being all too excited to help me plan my wedding as visions of spoiled grandbabies danced in her head.

The wedding was huge, and I over spent every penny of savings I had to make it all come together on Daytona Beach in Florida. My big day was so very stressful and emotional. Somehow I had forgotten my shoes in all the chaos, and my hairdresser had to lend me hers. They were a size too small and held my toes hostage in an unyielding vice grip the entire walk down the white paper covered, concrete aisle.

That wasn't the worst of it. My hairdresser had been divorced four times. Of all the omens that could plague one's wedding day, having to wear the shoes of a four-time divorcee had to be the worst! Still, Stephen and I were united man and wife on a beautiful Saturday in June in front of about 150 of our closest friends, family and fans as the Daytona Beach sun, sand and blue sky served as a memorable backdrop to our "Forever I Do's."

I had asked God to bless us and please allow us to get through the outdoor wedding without rain. He obliged, but I kid you not, the minute our pastor pronounced us "Man and Wife," loud thunder resounded, the sky quickly turned an eerie gray, and raindrops the size of Chiclets began to fall as our guests scurried inside on the tails of the recessional. I guess I should have known I was in for some stormy weather ahead. The clues

don't get any more obvious than that! I believe God by nature
is a whisperer, but when he decides to raise his voice, you know
without a doubt you are in big trouble!

Soon after, baby Andrew pushed his way into the world. Stephen and I had little time to actually enjoy the newness of being
husband and wife as the demands of parenting beat down our
door without rest. Meanwhile, we were struggling financially,
trying to live on Stephen's salary as I had to deal with a difficult
pregnancy, avoid complications of a threatening premature birth
and deal with hormonal mood swings that I often took out on
him. I felt fat and unattractive after trading my relatively ath-
letically toned body for 77-pounds of increase and a mirror that
always reflected me wearing a distorted Orca-whale-reversed-
camel suit I neither wanted nor recognized.

I knew things were headed south when two weeks after our
child was born, Stephen announced he had lost his job. He
had hidden the news for a few days because he was afraid of
upsetting me. Rather than go out immediately to look for new
work, he asked me in apparent despair what we were going to
do. I was nursing little "Drew" at the time and for a moment
I went numb. I watched as a tear that had silently rolled down
my left cheek fell on top of our baby's head. I couldn't even
move to wipe it.

I was on maternity leave without pay. We had already sunk to
depths I never imagined by having to sign up for our govern-
ment's Women, Infants and Children program. Daily I wrestled
with the flashback to my "Voted Most Likely to Succeed" high
school memory. "If they could see me now," I'd shamefully
mumble. "I'm fat, I'm broke, and I'm on WIC."

An Inevitable Parting

Our marriage was very rocky and we both knew it. Stephen
admitted he just wasn't ready to become a father so soon, and
I was beginning to realize that being married to my playmate

would not automatically make him my soul mate. Yet I was willing to do whatever it took to make our marriage work. I would
endure anything because my heart loved Stephen. I wanted the
best for our child and our little family, but my pride spoke loudest because I could not ever imagine being divorced.

WIC was one thing, but divorce was a whole new ballgame of
failure in my eyes. It didn't help that the Pastor at my church
continuously echoed how disappointing divorce was to God.
I compounded my already deteriorating feelings of self-worth
with this defeating spiritual doctrine. Soon, I found myself
plagued with virtually no self-esteem, daily attempting to hide
my depression from the outside world.

Just shy of three years into the marriage, divorce became
pressingly more inevitable. Stephen had become disenchanted
with the entire concept of marriage, fatherhood, responsibility
and most important, my constant nagging. I had fallen out of
love and into a tangled web of Stephen's lies, financial question
marks and the soul crushing uncovering of his year-long affair
with a co-worker. I could and had endured a lot, but I knew I
could not live with this ugly reality no matter how much praying, counseling or forgiving I would attempt.

It would be unfair and irresponsible not to accept my share
of blame in our marriage's demise. I really was a nag at times,
constantly wanting Stephen to grow up and be a provider. Stephen just wanted me to learn to chill out and enjoy life without
stressing over finances, parenting and my career. I had placed a
great deal of unfair expectation upon his shoulders.

I knew before we were married that I was always the "make
something new and exciting happen" kind of girl, vexed with
impatience and intolerance when the world did not move to the
beat of my drum. Stephen was a "laid-back, let life happen kind of
guy," who hated confrontation and admitted he lacked ambition
to do anything that required hard work. Perhaps it's why we were
so attracted to one another in an "opposites attract" fashion.

We failed on many levels to see eye- to- eye. Why we expected each other to be different just because we'd become husband and wife is beyond me. No wonder that thunder cloud hovered and haunted us so closely on our wedding day.

I had just gotten my big television break, having signed a six-figure contract with Fox Sports Net to anchor their Washington, DC sports broadcast. The day I found out about the affair, Stephen and I were packing up the house and having a huge yard sale preparing for our move from Jacksonville. Suddenly, I found myself only packing for two instead of three, and I did it through the eyes of a woman blinded not only by incessant tears, but the fear and confusion of what life would be like separated from Stephen and dealing with the esteem battles that were sure to follow.

It's odd because I had always been a very confident and bold woman believing and expecting the best of things. I had almost instantly become a pessimist, painfully depressed and miserably bitter about everything. I was sure I would never love again, I would never trust again, and I would never truly be happy as a single parent. Thanks to the rebound, I was wrong.

Self-concocted visions of the mistress I had never met and my choking the living daylights out of her and Stephen haunted my dreams. The stress of the sudden separation, anxiety over a new career and confusion over how I would care for two-year-old Andrew made all of my hair fall out...literally. It fell out daily in clumps as if I was undergoing mild chemotherapy. It also took 26 pounds off my frame in as little as four weeks. I barely ate and almost never slept, yet I tried to keep up the facade that life was treating me well and I was on top of the world.

I coped by locking myself in the bathroom so Drew couldn't see me for quick ten minute cries and then laughing at how ugly my expressions were in the mirror. I was like some sick psycho nutcase crying one minute then laughing the next. One time I forgot to lock the door and Drew came toddling in when I was in the midst of my hysterics. At the top of his lungs the poor boy screamed, "Mommy, nooooo, no cry, Mommy, noooo!" His outburst rang much louder than my own and slapped me into the reality that it was time to get a grip and move on.

My New Love

So I took a shot at marriage and I missed – bad! In fact, it proved to be the biggest air ball I'd ever shot in my life. The crazy thing is, even in the midst of all my pain and anguish, and a lot of things going dismally wrong, there were plenty of things suddenly going right. They were going right because I had prayed and trusted that eventually they would, but they were also going right because after the Drew outburst, I was determined to do whatever it took to rebound from this situation and live to take another shot – a better shot.

For the first time in my life I finally had the financial stability I desperately desired. I had the car of my dreams. And I bought my first home, independent of Stephen or anyone else. I looked good in my shiny, new, white Mercedes Benz SUV and my new wardrobe, four sizes removed. I took Drew with me virtually everywhere I went and hired temporary Nannies when I could not bring him along. I was living in this sudden dream world, even if I was living in it without a mate. It was just a matter of time before I found another I decided.

Over the next couple of years, I dated Zack the electrician, then Mark the 6'8" policeman, Sarge the short Army man, Tucker the Air Force Lieutenant who was as fine as they come and knew it, and Theodore, a dear old friend. I entertained a ridiculous e-mail flirtation with an old high school friend who was divorcing his wife and actually getting pointers from me.... *me* of all do-do birds in the jilted cage!

When all of these relationships and a few others I won't dare mention fell flat, I was a mess. I was spinning out of control. "Relationship Loser" was threatening to be my life title as I remained hungry and embarrassingly desperate to find love. Still, the more I failed at the dating game, the more determined I was to love again. I believed at some point I would surely be rewarded for my resiliency, even if I had already collected more rewards for stupidity and desperation.

Then one day it happened. I finally met someone I knew I could love unconditionally and who would reciprocate the same. Surprisingly, my true love proved to be a woman!

She was so much like me in every way. She even looked a lot like me, or at least the way I used to look when I was strong, confident, bold and beautiful. She was staring at me as if trying to look directly through my eyes and into the very soul of my existence. She seemed to know about my painful past, my foolish mistakes, my self-inflicted drama, my crippling inability to trust, my fears of inadequacy and insignificance, and she wanted to love me anyway. The beautiful woman I was falling head over heels for was – ME!

"Me" had come just when I needed "me" the most, and I have not stopped loving her for one moment since we were reunited that one fateful morning. Almost seven whole years I had hoped to find this beautiful "me" person. Somehow the "me" I'd lost was always there loving me, pushing me and wanting the best for me. I had spent so much time trying to avoid negative perceptions and loneliness, and placing cheap-date bandages over a broken-hearted stab wound, that I totally failed to notice she was there.

I placed my fears of what people thought, what people said and how I might be perceived over what I actually felt, needed and believed. I depended on everyone else's love and admiration when I should have always tried to put the love of "me" first.

My new love and I cried tears of joy that morning, so happy we had found each other. We made a pact we would never depart as friends and trusted advisors, no matter who or what came into our lives from that day forward...and so far so good.

I did a lot of shooting and missing at love only to discover I was aiming at the wrong goal. I should have been shooting at the goal that was right in front of me. Had I shot and scored there first, I would have prepared myself to be a much better player.

It is very difficult to be a strong team player when your individual skills are weak. It took a lot of heartbreak and agony, but I finally came to the realization that I had become a relationship loser only because I was no longer a self-love winner.

Inner Peace

Stephen and I are good friends now, something I could never imagine possible eight years ago. We've both grown a lot. We have a bond full of love and laughter tied together uniquely through our son. I've made peace with all of my past relationships and found peace within myself for my past mistakes. The long range shooter I've always been, I have come to accept that in life and in basketball, even if I'm deemed a good shooter, I will likely miss as many if not more times than I will score. However, the outcome of the game depends greatly on my willingness and ability to rebound.

I've also learned that while it's necessary to be assertive in going after the missed shot, it's not necessary to rush into shooting the follow up. Sometimes you just have to go up and get that ball, kick it back outside, take your time and set up a new offense. Rebounding should never mean forcing up another bad shot. It should mean creating the opportunity for a new and improved shot.

Strong rebounders are physically assertive and tough minded. Smart rebounders have the good court vision and court sense to know when it is time to go for the quick put back, and when it is time to reset the offense. It took some time for me to become both strong and smart because I was looking to be validated for my rebounding efforts with outside approval. Now I know strength and wisdom come from within.

In fact, the best basketball coaches in the world will tell you in order to be a relentless rebounder, you have to have heart. Experience has taught me that it is also true that in order to have heart (or mend a broken one), you have to be a relentless rebounder!

* * *

ON THE COURT....

Use Your Head and Your Heart

Survey almost any collegiate basketball coach, men's or women, and they will tell you they would be very pleased to have their teams with a field goal average of 45% – not 90%, not 75%, not even 50%, which is clearly considered "failing" by scholastic or academic standards. While a select few outstanding shooting teams will actually achieve making half their shots in an average season, it is far more common to have teams on average hover around 40%. No wonder so many coaches stress rebounding of the basketball.

Rebounding is one of the biggest keys to winning the game. Rebounds equate to possessions, and every possession of the basketball sets up the opportunity as well as the hope to score the most baskets and win the game. Players cannot expect to hit every shot. They are lucky to hit even half! Therefore, an immediate mindset of expectation must exist in every player to rebound the ball, as it is absolutely critical to the game.

So why do so many coaches have to repeat themselves over and over again? In every gym across the country you will repeatedly hear, "Box out! Rebound! Go after the ball!" The mathematics and the statistics are simple, "You will miss more times than you will make shots." Yet still, stock in Tums and Tylenol remain great investments, as coaches around the world suffer upset stomachs and headaches for trying to get this through their players' heads.

Aha! Perhaps there lies part of the problem. Rebounding is not simply about the head. It's about the heart. Players need more than an understanding of the simple statistics. They need the hunger that drives them toward the hope of winning. Then they need the heart to engage and assert themselves to go after that hope by rebounding the basketball on both the defensive as well as the offensive ends of the floor.

On the defensive end, far too many times, players fail to put themselves in position to rebound effectively by a concept known as "blocking out" or "boxing out" the opponent. This requires anchoring and squaring one's body in front of the opposing rebounder, making the physical contact to block out and push back, thus gaining a fair advantage to grab the ball when it comes off the rim. Instead, many players just turn and run after the ball and it flies over their head, or a stronger opponent pushes in or leaps higher to snag ball. In other words, fools rush in.

On the offensive end, a player or his teammate may take a shot, and rather than follow after the shot, determined to hawk down the ball and battle for possession that will offer a second chance to score, that player will stare into space as if in mesmerized or in deep reflection. There are likely a myriad of reasons why they do not pursue the rebound. Sometimes it's laziness ("I'm too tired to go after my shot."). Sometimes it's vanity ("That sure looked and felt like a good shot."). Sometimes it's self pity or frustration ("I can't believe I missed another shot!"). Most coaches care less about the reason but are sure of the remedy – a comfortable seat on the bench for that player to get a better view of the game!

Set Yourself Up for Success

Many times in life you will shoot and miss. You have to rebound! Wisely, courageously and relentlessly rebound that ball and set yourself up for another chance. It will rarely prove to be in your best interest to foolishly rush in to get the ball without securing yourself against the obstacles or opposition you may face. It is equally ineffective to just stand around and watch after you miss the shot, hoping somehow the ball will miraculously find its way back to your loving arms and you'll get another attempt.

Agonizing over a miss by no means should ever be an option, no matter how ugly the shot. It will never place you one step closer to making one. You didn't get the job offer? Rebound and apply for another one! You didn't make the grade you wanted? Study harder to be prepared for the next test. You didn't get the date you wanted to go to the prom? Perk up, dress up and take yourself! There's always another shot, another way or another opportunity if you rebound your misses! You will learn a lot about who you are by your willingness to rebound.

Don't get overly carried away with rebounding though. Remember the goal is and will always be to score. No one wants to spend a lifetime constantly rebounding misses and *never* scoring. Obviously, if this has been your struggle, you likely have to consider revamping your shot or your strategy. Maybe you need a little help. You may have to consider that you cannot rebound every shot alone. It's comforting to surround yourself with teammates whom you also can count on to rebound your miss. They will be equally comforted by your strong support. That's what teamwork is all about.

When I've been brokenhearted it usually has helped to talk with a good friend. When I've felt spiritually bankrupt, prayer and the church have always helped me cash in on a healthier perspective. My parents have always proven awesome advisors on job decisions, money matters and general life stuff. When I've been ill, mentally or physically beyond my own sensible care, I've sought professional medical help. Surrounding myself with a great team of rebounders has always helped me win in the long run.

There will be times, however when you do feel alone and no one can rebound from your mistake but you. Find confidence and comfort in knowing you really do have what it takes inside to try again. Remember, it is typical to miss more often than you make shots in the game. But you improve your chances of making those shots with the constant rebounding, refocusing and reattempting in practice.

There is a tendency for us to believe that we get once chance, one shot, and if we screw it up our whole world will come to an end. Now that is some serious pressure! While every shot is an important one, not every shot has to be your last. Yes, a particular shot or game may come to an end. Your season may even be over...but your whole world? I doubt it. So don't put that kind of pressure on yourself. Know that in the big picture there is always another chance, even if it means you will be shooting on another team, at another basket or in a different arena. The game of life goes on, so rebound and maximize your possessions and chances to score!

Without a doubt, at some point you will find yourself in a critical moment, at the end of the game with a last second shot on the line, or free throws allotted as time is about to expire that could win the game. The last thing you want to do is be panic stricken and shoot in desperation. I've been in those situations in life as well as on the basketball court. As nerve racking as those situations proved to be, I found comfort in knowing the odds were with me. I always figured all my previous misses were surely there to challenge and prepare me for this very moment.

Each shot missed mentally prepared me to train myself how to shoot a better shot. Each rebound I secured trained my heart to always be willing to try again. I also learned the frustration and negativity that often tried to tag along with those misses never got anything accomplished. Rebounding the ball meant I still had desire, and that desire empowered me to take and make the next shot.

So when the game is on the line, for me there was nothing left to do but take a deep breath, keep my elbow in, bend and extend, follow through and confidently visualize that shot going in. I had missed a lot of shots, so I had plenty of practice and preparation rebounding and trying again. I understood and embraced that now was the time to make that big shot, not panic. I became known as a pretty good clutch shooter, but not before I learned the value of being a strong rebounder.

As a point of mental focus, I tell players to shoot the ball like it's their last shot, but I remind them to rebound like they've been rewarded just enough time for one more. I believe shooting the ball is a measure of the mind and body's talent and skill. Relentlessly rebounding the basketball is more a measure of character, the heart's determination to persevere.

I am always most impressed by players who are not just great scorers, but awesome rebounders as well. This is true on the court as well as off. I want to know about your misses and how you rebounded from them. To me, that makes a more inspiring story than hearing you hardly ever miss a shot because you are so naturally gifted.

Some say basketball is mostly mental....I say I sure hope the rebounding heart never finds out!

DO WHAT'S NECESSARY:
Passionately Play Your Position

OFF THE COURT....

An Early Arrival

I had been on my feet all day trying to take advantage of every Christmas bargain sale advertised. When I returned home late Saturday evening and finally elevated my mammoth, swollen "cankles," it hit me. The pain in my pregnant belly cut like a machete, throbbing in bursts like small cannons exploding inside of me. Then it would subside. Minutes later it was back again, claiming dominance and ownership of every nerve ending in my abdomen.

Buckled over in pain, I leaned over to my husband and suggested he get me to the hospital right away. It was time. But it wasn't time. I knew it couldn't be time. It was the first week in December and Dr. Lomax assured me the little baby inside me was only in his 32nd week and not due to arrive until around the 22nd of January. Someone obviously forgot to send my baby the memo because he was surely trying to push his way into the world by any means necessary. The premature contractions I was experiencing were obviously his not-so-subtle way of letting me know he did not appreciate being overlooked.

"That damn Eve! It was just a stupid apple, woman! It's not like it was even caramel or chocolate covered or anything! Why couldn't you have been stronger, resisted the serpent's temptation and spared all of us women this horrific labor pain and drama?" I thought to myself as Stephen raced our car down the highway.

By the time we arrived at the hospital, the pain seemed unbearable. I was immediately taken into the emergency room and after what felt like a few thousand vaginal and abdominal pokes, urine and blood tests and an I-V hook up, it was immediately decided that baby Andrew would have to be prevented from coming into the world tonight because his lungs were underdeveloped and his premature birth could prove fatal. Meanwhile, the morphine drip or whatever kind of medication they had in that I-V burned like acid shooting through the veins in my right hand. I've always been a little embarrassed and reticent about public displays of agony, but there seemed to be no time like the present to let out one writhing scream after another at the top of my lungs praying for the pain to end.

Offering what seemed to be sincere, but totally ineffective concern over my condition, one nurse after another would come into the room where I was bawling uncontrollably and contorting my body in new and improved yoga positions trying to get the pain to subside. My husband stood helplessly in the corner, praying none of my calamity was contagious and wondering whether Satan had truly taken over the body of the woman about to give birth to his first child.

It took hours for the medicine to do what it was supposed to do. The goal was to retard the contractions and help keep little Andrew in his womb-room until medical science determined it was safe for him to come out and play. At some point I suppose I had finally cried myself to sleep. When I was fully coherent again it was the next morning and I had been moved to another room.

The new nurse advised me it was her understanding that I had a pretty rough night. "You don't say, Sherlock," I mumbled, the drugs and my sarcasm getting the best of me. Soon after my doctor arrived and advised me I would have to remain in the hospital indefinitely on complete bed rest as the slightest activity may set off little Andrew's insistence to enter the world before his time again.

There I lay with my legs elevated on pillows, as family, nurses and various food staff members made their regular visits to my room. I felt unreasonably bloated and helpless. I was constantly inundated with needles and bedpans and blood pressure readings. A natural type-A busy body, the hardest thing for me to do was to remain motionless for days, bored to tears, and stuffing my face with various snacks and goodies. (Actually, the snacks and goodies face-stuffing wasn't much trouble at all. I had become All-Pro in this sport, MVP even – Most Valuable Piglet!) Eventually, I was at least allowed to get out of bed to go to the restroom, but beyond that it was lie around, eat and sleep. I'm sure this would be a welcome vacation for some, but for me, it was a nightmare. On top of everything else, I was on leave without pay from work. Worry and frustration were reaching new heights.

A New Focus

My mother and father always said that from the moment I was born, I was never able to keep still. No wonder my child was trying to break out of confinement prematurely. The busy-body gene came honestly. Two weeks of non-movement in a hospital bed as I lay around agonizing about bills, Christmas gifts, and no paycheck was like cruel, cold-turkey therapy for me. I thought for sure I would go completely out of my mind. I was not the most gracious patient at first. Daily I would complain to my doctor and nurses about having to remain still in that dreaded bed, in that dreaded room.

"Dr. Lomax, I feel fine. This place is making me stir crazy! I'm ready to get back on the radio. You know, I had to take leave without pay. When can I get out of here and get back to work? Really, I feel much better. The contractions have totally stopped, right?" I reasoned and pleaded.

Tired of hearing my whining, Dr. Lomax gave me a pungent dose of "shut up and get over yourself."

She said, "Did you ever stop to think it's not about you, Vera? Have you forgotten that it's about you bringing a new life into this world? If you plan on doing that safely, if you plan on your baby surviving, you will lie in this hospital bed, and you will find peace in being still and getting rest, something you won't have very much of once the baby arrives. I suggest you try to appreciate the fact that because you are lying still in this hospital, you and that baby have a chance of living a happy life together. Your son's lungs are not healthy. The only chance he has at surviving and living a healthy, normal life depends on your ability to just be still until we determine it is safe for you to do otherwise." With that, Dr. Lomax offered a smug grin and walked out of the room.

New perspective and a bit of embarrassment and shame overwhelmed me. I was being asked to play a whole new position, not just in being still in a hospital bed so that I might have a healthy delivery, but in becoming a mother altogether. Perhaps eight months of carrying around an extra load, swollen ankles, sore back, and uncontrollable eating binges had taken its toll on my psyche. I had ballooned an additional 70 pounds at this point and there were so many things that seemed to ignite hormonal stress levels I had never experienced before.

I was thrilled at the thought of finally becoming a mother, but I sure wasn't acting like it. I was focused on not feeling attractive, not liking so many changes to my body, and not feeling very secure about being a new mother. Pregnancy was so tough. Being a mother was sure to be tougher. Yet I was chosen to become a mother, and no matter how difficult that process would prove to be at times, I realized my attitude and gratitude was in need of a complete overhaul.

"For Heaven's sake, V, don't you get it? You're about to bring a whole new life into the world! My little baby is depending on me for his survival. His life depends on me!" my mind echoed. What an honor and privilege this was, yet I was lying around feeling selfish and sorry for myself. I was being asked to be still. I wasn't asked to run a marathon or move a mountain with my pinky finger; I was asked to simply rest and be still. My baby's life depended on it. How hard was that really?

My Leo the Lion pride kicked in and suddenly nothing was more important than saving this little baby's life. Nothing in the entire world was more important to me. I was going to be a mother, and I was determined to be a good one. No, I was determined to be a great one. I was so thankful to Dr. Lomax for waking me up. I was thankful to God for the awesome responsibility He had placed before me. I promised if He let this little baby be born healthy, I would do everything in my power to place him first and I would try my hardest to never ever again complain. I was thankfully blessed and I never wanted to appear selfish this way again.

The Greatest Gift

Two weeks later I was released from the hospital. I was allowed light-to-moderate activity. I returned to my Program Director duties at the radio station but conducted most of my job from a seated position and learned to delegate a lot more. I prepared the station as best as I could for my upcoming absence. Everyone commented on how much I seemed to glow, how rested and peaceful I seemed. I told them I was. I felt great and I was excited about the awesome new responsibility that awaited me. I was no longer scared, frustrated or agonizing over my pregnancy. I was ready now, really ready to become Supermom!

A week later, I had a well-baby visit in Dr. Lomax's office. It was then that she let me know little Andrew was still trying to get into this world a bit earlier than expected. I was already beginning to dilate. I was three centimeters, whatever that meant in obstetrics talk. All I knew is she decided to induce labor that day and said she fully expected sometime within the next 24 hours I would start feeling the contractions again.

"No, not the dreaded contractions. Anything but that pain again!" I internally panicked. (So much for that whole being really ready part!) Quickly I caught myself and remembered how I promised to not be a complete whiner about anything related to the whole child birthing thing again.

"Okay little baby, let's do this thing!" I sighed to myself. I went home, had a giant meal, and waited anxiously for my big moment.

It was 3:00 a.m. when I felt the first contraction. I woke up Stephen and told him this time it was the real thing. We were going to have our baby! It was a sweet, tender moment that lasted about five seconds as another contraction came knocking. Somewhere between that announcement and arriving at the hospital emergency room, that demon possessed monster had taken over my nerve endings in my body and I was once again in extreme pain. I tried to keep reminding myself that soon it would be over and a beautiful baby would be born. I just had to be courageous and strong.

My mother and father arrived at the hospital as soon as possible, having to drive a couple of hours from their home. It was amazing how everyone just assumed their positions, doing their best to mask their anxiety and offer their support. Stephen stayed right by my side as I occasionally hurled insults, blame and language about his getting me into this predicament that made my poor mother blush.

Mom read the Bible and fed me ice chips. My father positioned himself down the hall in the waiting room. He'd popped his head in only once after arriving and likely after seeing me look like a wild-haired, stuffed gargoyle decided immediately this room would be no place for him. I'm sure Daddy's little girl looked anything but. Always the wisest man, he knew to get as far away from that room as possible!

The night would go on to include many dramatic moments. The worse of which involved a sweaty and nervous intern sent to give me an epidural. Mr. Butterfingers slipped when he pricked my lower back, missing his intended target and causing an unexpected spinal tap. I couldn't move or feel anything from my neck down. I lie in this state of paralysis sucking ice chips for hours. Suddenly, without warning, the anesthesia wore off and my body went from complete numbness to the complete agony of insufferable, rapid contractions all over again.

Sixteen hours had passed in total. It was time. Dr. Lomax and her nurses arrived in their Latex gloves and mouth masks with their baby-birthing game faces on. The doctor was telling me to push, Stephen was trying to help me breathe the way we learned in Lamaze class, Mom was holding my hand until I squeezed it too tight and she screamed like she was having the baby. From that point, hand holding was Stephen's job and Mom became the quiet, bulging eyed, prayer supporter at the end of the bed.

I was exhausted from the labor and understood nothing except why it was called "labor." I had been pushing for what seemed an eternity. I insisted I couldn't push anymore. I just wanted to sleep now, you know, lay still like the first time I was in the hospital. "Couldn't we just go back to that whole bed rest thing and let the food staff bring me some catfish and mashed potatoes? Umm, I sure would love some catfish and mashed potatoes now." I was delirious. I was trying to think of anything except this barbaric, natural childbirth pain.

The doctor kept telling me I had to bear down and push. Stephen would echo the orders. Sweat pouring from my brow, I told them both where they could go push their darn selves. I was so tired and so weak and so hungry and it all hurt so badly!

Why had I been forsaken? Why was everyone picking on me and yelling at me to push?

"I can see the head!" Dr. Lomax declared.

"Then pull it out!" I shot back. What the heck did she think this was? I didn't need her play-by-play; just pull the darn thing out! The room was spinning. I thought for sure I was ready to throw up.

"You have to give me one really big push, Vera. Bear down and give me everything you have."

"I did already! I can't, Doctor, I can't. Please just use them salad prong things or that plunger and pull this baby out! Hell, crawl in there and get him if you have to! I just can't push! I have nothing left." I was tired of her giving the orders. I wanted to be the boss. I earned it!

She reasoned, "You give me one big last push, Vera and I'll pull. Stephen, you tell her when, count down to the contraction. Mom, wipe her brow."

Everyone had their job. We were all in position. The suction cup thing was on baby's head.

"3-2-1, PUSH!" Stephen yelled. The pain hit and I pushed so hard I was sure I had turned my entire body inside out. I let loose a deep, guttural, primal scream that awakened the dead in every cemetery within a 75-mile radius of Fort Pierce Memorial.

"He's out, V! You did it! You did it! It's a boy!" the doctor said gleefully.

In the distance I heard a faint tiny cry. Then I felt Stephen fall on top of me crying all over me. I caught Mom out my peripheral vision on the other side of the bed clasping her hands over her mouth as a tear rolled down her face. But I still didn't see the baby. All that screaming and pushing, where was the baby? I tried to put the words together. It took all I could muster,

"Wh-wh-where's my baby?" I managed in breathy anxiety.

Just then, a little white towel with pink and blue stripes was headed toward me from Dr. Lomax's hands, and she placed in my arms and this little, pink, yellow and white spotted Asian-eyed, wet, black-haired, warm bundle. He opened one eye as if to wink at me in mischievous, self-admission that he knew he had caused me quite a devilish stir. Then he wiggled around a bit trying to get more comfortable as his mouth popped open and I thought he might say, "Hey, Ma! What's up?" Yet he said nothing audibly.

What my spirit heard him say was, "I'm so happy to finally be here and meet you, lady. Thank you for not giving up on me. I know it wasn't easy to get me here. You're awesome and I love you!"

He was the most beautiful funny-looking little thing I had ever seen in my life. I told him his name was Andrew – Andrew Verán. Andrew was his father's middle name and it meant "strong," and Verán was made up from my first name, Vera, meaning "faith."

Instantly all the pain I endured had disappeared and my soul was filled with a passion and a purpose I had never known. "Strong faith" was born of me. I had been given the blessing of new life. It was an unbelievable moment of selflessness, purpose and creation. At that very moment, I knew nothing in the entire world mattered more to me.

"Drew" as I call him, is almost eleven now. He's a fifth grade, straight A student who may very well be one of the most genuinely passionate and happy kids on the planet. He couldn't wait to get here for a reason. You need only meet him once and catch a glimpse of his contagious smile to know he's a pretty special and blessed little guy. He has endured battles with his lungs and a hearing impairment, yet never once have I ever heard him complain. His passion for life always seems to get him through the toughest of times.

While it is true that I brought Andrew into a whole new life, I find just as great significance in the fact Andrew brought a whole new life to me. It is a life graciously filled with purpose and passion, and a life indeed of "strong faith."

* * *

ON THE COURT....

Do What's Difficult

Last year, Andrew was the second shortest player on his youth basketball team. The coach played him in both the point guard and shooting guard positions. This season, having enjoyed a twelve pound and three-inch growth spurt in a year, he has found himself to be the second tallest player on the team and in unfamiliar territory playing in the post. What's great about Andrew is he doesn't seem to favor one position or the other. He just wants to know what he is supposed to do and he wants to be good at it.

I love that about that boy and I'm convinced he'll go far because of it. He's got that special enthusiasm about learning and performing that is rare to find. Perhaps it's because he's an only child and hasn't spent a lot of time trying to compare himself to competitive siblings. Or maybe it's just because he's too young to really care very much about positions or perceptions. He did, however, once ask me what the most important position on the team was.

Not trying to sound political, flaky or yielding, I of course said they were all equally important. I added, however that there was one position that I believed to be the most difficult to play.

"Is it the point guard, because he is the one who has to run the offense and handle the ball the most?" he asked.

"No, that's a tough position, but not the toughest," I answered.

"Is it the center, because all the defenses are fouling him in the key and he has to get all the rebounds?" he continued.

"No," I chuckled at his simplistic and innocent evaluation of the center's floor duties.

"Then what do you think, Mom?" He was tired of guessing.

"I think the most difficult position to play is the one when you're sitting on the bench. The second most difficult position to play is your own."

"Huh?" Andrew's head cocked to the side and he gave me the "I'm just a kid; why must you make everything so complicated" look.

I went on to explain to Andrew that the hardest position we are asked to play in basketball is the one when we don't get to play. We far too often overlook the importance of being a bench rider. It isn't a position we enjoy, but if it is the position we've been asked to play, we need to learn to play it as passionately and intensely as if we were asked to be the starting point guard or the center of attention.

We tend to take for granted that there is value in being still, sitting, watching and learning the game while cheering on our teammates. We fail to realize that although this is not the position we aspire to, it is still a position of extreme importance. It is the position where we cultivate our greatest hunger to do more, to contribute more and to feel a greater sense of purpose while simultaneously learning patience.

The result should be a player who is more open to constructive criticism, who gains greater perspective and who competes harder in practices. I said this is what it should be, but in truth, riding the bench gets my vote for the most difficult to play because few players can perform this position passionately.

Life holds for us this same struggle. Have you ever had to wait your turn for that huge promotion, pay raise or advancement opportunity of any kind that you thought you rightfully deserved? Well, then you know how difficult it is to sit on the bench. The longer you sit on that bench, the easier it becomes to pout, place blame, have self-doubt, worry, covet and contemplate giving up, if not actually doing so altogether.

How about in your social or love life when you feel so confidently you have done everything necessary to put yourself in position to meet a Mr. or Mrs. Right, who never seems to show up? What about the athlete that has performed at the top of his game only to sustain a season-ending injury and be forced to watch from the sidelines? Being on the bench rarely ever seems fair. It rarely ever feels very good. But what if you could pour all your passion into the possibilities of growth and preparedness that can only come from being on that bench? How great, how ready, how awesome and complete a player might you be then?

The Perfect Player

Marie, my first recruit at my first Division One assistant coaching job at the University of Dayton called me recently. She was breathlessly ecstatic.

"Coach V, you will never believe what happened to me! I had the most important, most magnificent, most perfect game of my career! I had a career high 19 points! I was 8-8 from the field and 3-3 from the free throw line. I couldn't miss tonight! I didn't miss a single shot! The newspapers did a big article on me and everything! I just wish you could have been there!"

I would have loved to have been there and would likely have been crying like a proud mother at graduation. Marie had come a very long way. A native of Africa, she stood about 6-feet 2-inches, and was a long, lanky, prototypical track athlete. She had only started playing basketball as a sophomore in high school when she began attending school in the United States.

She was a great athlete, but her basketball knowledge and talent were extremely raw. She was an enthusiastic and extremely adept learner who humbly realized she had a lot to do to make the basketball grade, which made her all the more coachable and revered. She understood and accepted why she did not play in the majority of games her freshman year, and she held great optimism about the next season.

Although she showed signs of improvement as a sophomore, Marie still wasn't getting off the bench very much and often became frustrated easier. Marie was an honor student who spoke six languages. She couldn't believe how long it was taking her to get a competitive edge and firm grasp on the game of hoops.

It was difficult to find someone to outrun or outwork Marie in practice. She put in the extra hours for individual workouts and shooting around by herself. Still as a junior, she was overlooked for the starting nod. Many games she struggled to get much playing time at all. This season, as a senior, her one highlight was that the coach who recognized her work ethic over the years named her team captain.

I received a long distance call that day as well, when she was tabbed with the team captain honor. She was proud that her work ethic had gotten noticed, but I could hear it in her voice that she still yearned for her basketball talents to have a chance to shine as brightly on the court. Averaging only about 10-15 minutes a game from off the bench, it was difficult for her to get that kind of opportunity. One fated night, she finally got her wish, and she delivered a perfect game that set new records at the University of Dayton in a thrilling victory for her team.

It would appear to the outsider Marie was an overnight success. Far from it! In three-and-a-half seasons, she had to endure the dreaded "bench time." Like contractions, something inside her felt ready to give birth to greatness, but the labor was long and painful. Unlike many who may have quit, Marie stayed true to her passion and her belief that sooner or later her time would come, and likely none too soon. Upon that time, she did not deliver what would be deemed a good or even a great game. Marie delivered a perfect one!

There was no way anyone could predict that it would have played out the way it did. Marie stayed true to what was in her control, and that was to maintain her passion for basketball regardless of being on the bench all that time. That passion would push her to work harder in practices. That passion would drive her to selflessly cheer for her teammates. That passion would motivate her to put in extra hours on her shooting in the gym. That passion would teach her to become a leader by example, with teammates and coaches respecting and admiring her resilience and maturity in waiting her turn to contribute, and doing what was asked to play a more humbling role so that the team was elevated above her individual success.

At some point, Marie came to realize being on the bench was all about being ready – not just thinking she was ready, and not simply saying she was ready – but actually being ready, mind, body and soul.

Every bench rider soon finds out that at some point you do get a chance to get in the game, and you have to make the absolute best of that moment. Many get that chance and they panic. Others have spent so much time being bitter that it's hard for any time off the bench to taste very sweet or to perform free of that bitterness.

We don't always fully understand that the coach, especially our Ultimate Coach, has a plan for us. We don't always yield to accept no matter how good, how smart, how talented, how loveable or how ready we think we are, we still have something more to learn from being on the bench in our various positions in life. We just want off the bench and into the game. We feel entitlement, and perhaps to some degree, we are entitled, but we are not in control. The only thing we can control is how we choose to perform in the position we are being asked to play at present, not the one we hope to play in the future. But know that your passion for the present position is directly related to how you will perform in the one you aspire to. Therefore, be passionate about growing, learning, being. The joy is in the journey, even when the journey doesn't seem to be moving quite as fast as you want it to.

Stay True to Your Role

I said earlier that the second most difficult position to play is our own. The point guard, the shooting guard, the small forward, the power forward and the center, also known respectively as the 1,2,3,4, and 5 players, all have important positions to play. So do the substitutes, the coaches, the referees, the water boy, the managers, the cheerleaders and the scorekeepers. They are all important to the game in one facet or another. Even the popcorn and soda vendors get a nod for importance in my book! We all have a position to play.

The position we play today may not be the same one we are asked to play tomorrow. Whatever the position, we perform far more effectively if we understand our individual roles and perform those related tasks with passion. For many of us, this is difficult to do because we are far too focused on someone else's position. We want someone else's position, playing time, girlfriend, job, sex appeal, money, status, etc. Our position isn't good enough, visible enough or not rewarded enough, so we sit around complaining and coveting instead of believing and achieving.

I am the first to advise anyone to go after what you want in life with great enthusiasm. But be sure you understand why you want it. If you only want it because someone else has it or someone else does it or anything related to your comparisons with someone else, you set yourself up for failure. You have to want it because you are purely passionate about it.

I truly believe **the purpose of pursuing your passion is to put passion back into your purpose.** When we deeply desire something, we go after it with an energy that attracts us to the truth about why we are here. Not to spoil it for everyone, but the reason is less about you than you think. You've ultimately been given gifts, talents and purpose to help others, but it's necessary for you to be passionate about those gifts and talents to figure out how you are best capable of doing so. You are unique and special, so comparing yourself and coveting what others have is pointless.

Play your position the most passionate way you can, whether it is as the team's leading scorer or the best practice player. If you fail to find pure passion and contentment in what you are doing then what you've learned at the very least is maybe you need to be doing something else. But if you give up before you have given it all of your passion, you may be passing up a critical opportunity to learn something very special about who you are and what purpose you serve.

Open yourself up to the true power of potential and purpose. Sometimes we find it on the bench. Other times we find it as the star of the game. But we seldom find it comparing ourselves to others. Rather, we find it giving our best to others. And we are only able to do that when we give our passionate best to ourselves.

I tell my son and players everywhere to know your role, appreciate your position, and when that position changes, know your new role and appreciate your new position. Most important, whatever your position, play it with passion, even if you don't fully understand your purpose or the trials or pain you may have to endure to find your purpose. Give birth to your strong faith that you are here for a very special reason. No matter what position you find yourself playing, that truth should sustain your passion for life.

STAND UP FOR WHAT'S RIGHT:
Defend Your Goal

OFF THE COURT....

An Opponent by Any Other Name...

Myrtle Beach, S.C., 1994 – I was living alone in a small home I was renting about ten miles away from the beach. I was 28 years old, relatively new to this deep, southern tourist town, working as a morning show co-host for a country radio station. Yes, I was a black woman chilling with the sounds of Reba McEntire, Garth Brooks and Shania Twain and loving it as "Bobbi Jones."

I always found it amusing how listeners would set up this beautiful, buxom, blond and blue-eyed visage of "Bobbi," and then get a true glimpse of "Vera" and exclaim in complete surprise, and sometimes disappointment, "She's black!"

"More of a caramel, actually," I'd shoot back in my "Bobbi Jones" southern drawl, chuckling as I walked away.

Some of my family members and friends thought I was taking a risk in my career as well as in my personal safety to take on the position. After all, this was the same South Carolina where racial disputes over the flying of the Confederate Flag at the

State House regularly made front page news. This was the same town where a pick-up truck purposely drove close to the edge of the uncurbed road where I was walking my dog, and a man on the passenger side in a white cut-off T-shirt hung out the window, spat at me and screamed, "Nigger, take your black ass back to Africa!"

Now, I wouldn't know how to get to Africa if I tried. What a silly thing to say! Despite this all, I made up my mind I was staying in Myrtle Beach and I was staying "Bobbi Jones" as long as I enjoyed what I was doing…and as long as the ratings continued to indicate the rest of the non-ignorant inhabitants and listeners desired to have me there. In fact, my morning co-host Marv Clark and I went on to win the "Personality of the Year" Award from the South Carolina Broadcasters Association as our radio station also moved on to become the top ranked station in the market.

I had reserved relatively no fear for the acts of racial ignorance or intolerance. I had saved all my shrieks of panic and hysteria for something far more intimidating: the Palmetto Bug, alias, *Periplaneta Americana*. For those of you who may be unfamiliar with the Palmetto Bug, please allow me to explain this insect to you in more picturesque detail.

The Palmetto Bug is the largest pest species of cockroach in the world, very common to tropical places, especially the southeastern United States. While prevailing in nature in various sizes, Palmetto Bugs can reach the length and width of an average adult male thumb. They are notorious for spreading bacteria, so they are equally as nasty as they are hideous. These gigantic, foul smelling, vile cockroach critters come in varying shades of brown with huge wings to fly into the most unwanted places.

Like all roaches, they believe in home ownership as a sacred family rite of passage. If you don't discourage them otherwise, the home they will seek to own will be *yours*! Swiftly scampering and crawling wherever they please, they are known to engage in late night snacks in your kitchen or dining room, sipping like fine wine the Raid Insect Spray you believed might actually kill them, and showering in your bathroom.

What I did not know – and I have to brace myself now to even think about it – is that they also enjoy cozying up in your bedroom! Unfortunately, I know these particular facts about the steroid-enhanced roaches from a very painful personal experience.

Getting Buggy

One ominous evening, wearing my then typical gym shorts and T-shirt pajamas, I settled into bed for what I had hoped would be a relaxing evening. I propped myself up on some pillows against the headboard, stretched my legs out and prepared to read a good book. I knew it wouldn't be long before my 4 a.m. alarm sounded and Bobbi Jones would need to wake up and once again entertain the country music faithful. Fate would have it that this night I was the one due to be entertained.

Engrossed in my book, I felt something suddenly plop down on my bare, right inner thigh. Startled, I quickly glanced down from my book only to discover it was the wretched Palmetto Bug that had come for story time! In half a blink, I screamed at the top of my lungs while flicking the unwanted beast off my leg. I flung the book across the room, sprung to a standing position on top of the bed, ran in place using the sprinter's high-knee technique, jumped down to the floor, turned abruptly to run and "Wham!"

I blindly crashed forehead first into the outer edge of my bedroom door. Meanwhile, the obstinate Palmetto Bug continued to sit on the bed watching me make a complete fool of myself. I imagined he soon scampered off to the kitchen as the virtual action-packed movie scene he just witnessed warranted some popcorn crumbs.

The adrenaline rush from the scare sustained me through the fat lip and egg-sized knot on my forehead, as well as the subsequently painful concussion. I stayed awake the entire night sitting straight up in a chair, nursing my headache, and jumping out my skin at anything I imagined was moving. I typically don't scare very easily, but for some reason that cursed, steroid-enhanced cockroach had me believing I might need clinical therapy. It was weeks before I could get a solid night of sleep without trembling. And it would take years before I could actually overcome my Palmetto Bug fear.

It would take another major, disturbing and frightening encounter before I would learn to stand up for myself and defend my home and sanity against this nasty enemy.

Ten years after my first face-to-face encounter with the Palmetto Bug, I had become an older, assumedly wiser woman living in Jacksonville. I had recently moved into a townhome in a new condominium community that was built in a heavily wooded area with a stream nearby. Due to the recent housing market recession, the townhome sat vacant for a year and a half. Well, vacant if you're not counting the Palmetto Bugs and spiders that I was unaware had secretly taken up residence. Surely you have heard of the adage that history has a funny way of repeating itself? Well, the Palmetto Bugs must have clearly been preparing to laugh again at my expense.

Having spent the previous decade living in parts of the Northeast and the Midwest, I had forgotten all about my *steroidalcockroacaphobia*. (Yes, I made this term up. I just thought giving my Palmetto Bug fear a clinical sounding name would grant my over-the-top fright reactions some justification!) I was no longer exposed to the threat of intimidating, concussion-causing bugs. Once back in the Southeast, however, in a highly populated area for insects, I began to have regular nightly and early morning encounters with Palmetto Bugs in our home.

Each encounter included my hysteric "Scream, Dance and Run" workout routine. Shamefully, I had resorted to asking my nine-year-old son, Andrew, to kill the bugs for me. Andrew, who inherited most of his looks and traits from his father, unfortunately inherited his fear from me. He proved to be better at the

"Scream, Dance and Run" workout than even I was! Poor boy! Finally, one fateful night, I decided it was time to fight. It was time to stop being a wimp and start being a woman of valor. The straw had broken the camel's back. Who knew I'd be that poor camel?

Lying in bed, I was talking on the phone to my boyfriend John, when I suddenly felt a tickling sensation on my left forearm, which was propped behind my head. I moved my arm as I cut my eyes into peripheral view to see what was causing the itch.

Jumping Jehosephat! It was another wretched, uninvited Palmetto Bug!

This time I was so alarmed, I simultaneously flicked the bug off my arm and flung my cell phone down the hallway with poor John's voice in the descending echo of "Are you O-o-o-k-k-k?" flying into a wall. In one motion, I vaulted to a standing position on top of the bed and screamed like I was auditioning for the next Halloween movie sequel! My heart was racing uncontrollably. I began flinging the sheets up and down over my head, snapping it so hard, so rapidly and so wildly, I pulled a muscle in my upper back and chest. I clinched at my chest as tears flooded my cheeks.

I couldn't move! But I had to, because despite all that flicking and flinging and screaming, the flippant cockroach was still on the bed! I screamed again and lunged off the bed, clasping my chest. It hurt so bad, I was convinced I was having a heart attack! I did the high-knee, tippy-toe run across the floor to the bathroom. I found some Excedrin and took it immediately. I had heard once if you were having a heart attack, you should take aspirin. I also heard "stupid is as stupid does" from the movie Forrest Gump. Boy, was I stupid right now.

I left that scene still not knowing where the Palmetto Bug ended up, and once again I was too paranoid to get back in my own bed to go to sleep. I immediately started recalling the entire first Palmetto Bug encounter in Myrtle Beach and how I had caused myself a concussion. I remembered my co-workers at the radio station wondering if I was in an abusive relationship when they saw the bruised knot on my forehead. I felt like a complete idiot telling everyone "a bug scared me." They all looked at me like, "Yeah, right, Bobbi, likely story."

I became very angry at myself for now having caused myself a muscle sprain that felt like a heart attack in my chest and back. "How stupid is it to be this much afraid of a bug?" I asked myself. "But it's a really big bug," I reasoned back. Meanwhile, I thought of Poor John, as he must have been worried to death. Somewhere his voice lingered in electronic space on the other end of a cell phone that had crashed into the wall and now lay broken and disassembled, with the battery out of its compartment halfway down the hall.

What a mess I had caused in so little time over a cursed cockroach! I was disgusted with myself. "I'm a grown woman, for God's sake!" I chastised myself. Oh, I was really mad now. The time had come to fight back. Why it took me so long to do so is beyond me.

Protecting My Turf

At the first light of day, I called my dad. An old country boy, he has never been afraid of bugs of any kind. He's not even afraid of snakes. I can't actually remember my father ever being afraid of anything. He's always been my hero and I trusted him to tell me what to do. Of course, he got a good chuckle out of hearing my little tale of complete hysteria, but then he immediately referred me to an exterminator who he said was very thorough.

I was on the phone with Mike, the exterminator, at 9 a.m. sharp. By 10 a.m. he was at my front door and I felt confident that those Palmetto Bugs were about to feel my wrath! They'd be sorry for ever messing with Bobbi Jones, I mean, Vera Jones, and any other Joneses from this day forward. I was in a full court press against these corrupt critters and I wouldn't let up until the ball was back in my court and I had won this game!

Then I put on my best zone defense. Mike explained to me other things I should do, like get all the cardboard boxes out of my garage as roaches love wet cardboard and tend to hang out in bunches there. Mike put me on a regular extermination schedule and explained to me how I would begin to see a lot of bugs and spiders in the house but promised me they would all be dead when I did. It was part of the process and a good way for me to know the chemicals were working.

I became a sick madwoman. I'd celebrate every time I saw a dead bug, screaming at its corpse, "Bring it on La Cucaracha! You want a piece of me, huh?" My son was always amused, but I think he was secretly concerned his mama might be turning a bit sadistic. Still, I was energized by my defensive plans working so effectively. I didn't have to be afraid anymore because I gained confidence in acquiring the knowledge and the power to defeat the little evil one!

Mike the exterminator was right. There were plenty of Palmetto Bugs in the garage. (They were dead ones, now! Hah!) I replaced all the boxes with plastic bins. I was sure to never leave food out uncovered at anytime and became obsessed with every crumb dropped. Poor Andrew probably never enjoyed another snack in the house from that day forward. I made him aware of the likelihood to see more bugs if he dropped any crumbs from his Doritos or Cheetos or Fritos or Cheerios. The boy was always eating something with O's.

I never again ate or drank anything in my bedroom except water. I was in complete defense mode. It's one thing to be caught off guard by something frightening. It's another to be educated about that which frightens you and still make stupid mistakes not to defend or protect yourself from its unwanted threat of annoyance or harm.

It's not healthy to live life in fear or paranoia of what might happen or what harm could occur. And by no means should anyone ever be as afraid of anything as I was of the Palmetto Bug. I will be the first to admit my fear was a bit irrational. I can't explain why I was so afraid. I guess I got caught so off guard the first time I encountered the bug on my thigh, and my response and reaction in turn caused so much pain, I psychologically somehow allowed that pain to be associated with Palmetto Bugs in general. I just decided I hated those gross creatures and I wanted nothing to do with them. They frightened the senses out of me.

When I finally came to my senses, I realized fear was doing me absolutely no justice. I decided whatever fear I had, I was not going to allow anything or anyone to upset the peace and sanctity of home. Home is that one place where I want to escape the things that "bug" me. By no means do I want to allow the bugs in to ruin that. Defense would prove to be my best offense when seeking to reach my goal of peace in the threat of the Palmetto Bug.

No matter how hard you work, how hard you try, how good a person you are or wish to be in life, there will always be little annoyances that seek to bug you. There are so many times when we can be courageous and wise and simply carry out the necessary steps to exterminate that which bugs us. Yet too many times, our fear responses take over and we end up reacting wildly and unwisely, often making a mountain out of a molehill, or in my case, a concussion out of a cockroach.

Even though I do not like or want Palmetto Bugs around me, they may still try to manipulate their way into my home and my life. They are natural inhabitants of the area in which I live. I can accept that. What I will not accept is not defending myself and causing myself pain rather than the repulsive insect because I was too uncourageous and unprepared to defend myself properly. Although I may never prove to be the bug-killing type that my father is, who kills Palmetto Bugs and bees with his bare hands (the apple rolled far from the tree on that issue), I do know how to roll up a newspaper or grab a shoe and squash one if I quickly need to now. I usually need a breath of fresh air and a gag bag after I do, but I get the job done!

Today I take all the precautionary measures with the disposal of food and cardboard and not leaving doors open for the bugs to scamper in when they want to. I know now that I need not be afraid, just smart, aware and ready to defend my home, my position, my sanity. I know how to call an exterminator for prevention or back up, whichever the situation requires. This defensive mentality has gotten me a long way. I have but one major goal in my home and that is to be at peace, and I'm ready to defend that with everything I am.

I pity the bug that's got to find out the hard way.

* * *

ON THE COURT....

The Power of Defense

"What kind of basketball coach doesn't even use basketballs?" I complained under my breath. A few of my teammates mumbled in agreement and disdain.

"The kind of coach that needs to teach you an important lesson about defense," Coach Fran shot back.

I swear she had supersonic dog ears that could hear what I was thinking before I even said a word!

"There is another part of this basketball game that you all don't seem to know very much about," she continued. "It's called defense. Some of you don't seem to think it is nearly as important as offense. I know you don't because you don't play like it, Vera!"

I hated when Fran called my name, and she always seemed to be calling my name. Fran was our assistant coach and defensive specialist at Syracuse University. I wanted to hand her the roster so she could memorize a few of the other players' names and not favor mine so much.

"Positions!" she bellowed and then continued, "Defensive Slides!" Then she blew that loathsome whistle that my entire Syracuse Orangewomen team prayed nightly she would lose in the trash, drop in the toilet or suddenly swallow one day.

"Tweet!" the whistle sounded and down we went from our standing position into our defensive stance, knees bent, feet shoulder length apart and arms extended out high and wide to the sides.

"Tweet!" Fran then moved her hands into a drumming motion to indicate she wanted us to quickly stomp our feet against the floor while still in our defensive stance.

"Tweet!" Fran pointed left and we followed her lead staying low in our stance and quickly sliding left.

"Tweet!" Fran pointed right so we slid back to the right.

"Tweet!" Fran gave direction for us to sprint forward.

"Tweet!" Now we had to slide diagonally backwards.

"Tweet!" Forward again.

"Tweet!" Stationary foot stomps again.

"Tweet, Right!"

"Tweet, Left!"

"Tweet, Front!"

"Tweet, Back!"

"Tweet, tweet, tweet, tweet – somebody kill this woman!" I'd think.

Since Fran could hear me thinking, she purposely blew that cursed whistle another minute longer screaming, "Come on, Vera, push yourself! Work harder!" as every muscle in my upper thigh, my kneecaps and lower back screamed obscenities. Finally she got to the final whistle blow, which euphorically meant we could rest and shake off what she told us was lactose burning in our legs.

"Lactose? That's the stuff in milk, right? I will never drink milk again!" I secretly swore to myself.

"Tweet!" After only about ten seconds of rest, she blew the whistle again, and the quick stomping of feet began again.

"Tweet...." This went on at nauseam, literally, for some players. I absolutely hated defensive slides. No wonder I never played any defense. What was there to like about defense or the grueling drills Fran put us through to make us better at it? I just decided I had no interest in being better if it had to hurt that way every day. After all, I was "Sweet V from the Top of the Key" not "Sweet V who loves to play D."

There would be days when my coaches were so frustrated with our team, seemingly me in particular, because we never seemed to grasp the importance or the significance of what Coach Barbara Jacobs would tell us over and over again that "Offense wins games, but Defense wins championships." Me, being the over analytical type, found comfort in my resolve that my evil coaches clearly didn't know what they were talking about, because that made absolutely no logical sense. A championship is still a game. So if offense wins games, and a championship is a game, then offense also wins championships. It's like the transitive property of mathematics, if a=b, and b=c, then a=c, don't you know that? Duh, my coaches didn't know anything!

Oh, I was so smart and so cynical about it all. All players always think they know more than the coaches. I know this to be fact from being on both sides of that equation now. I could appreciate the moans and groans I would get when I was coaching and conducting defensive drills with players in the past. Yet it was my experienced conviction of "they know not what's good for them yet" that made me push them even harder than Fran pushed me and the rest of my Syracuse teammates.

For the record, we won two Big East Championships while I was a player at Syracuse University. However, it probably wasn't until we did that I actually understood that my coaches weren't demonically possessed when they pushed us so hard in practice to be better defenders. They just wanted us to play like we were possessed.

Barb Jacobs, Fran Clemente, Mavis Washington and Kathleen Parker, I thank you for putting up with me when I knew not what it all meant. As a team, and as individuals, they needed us to gain the mental and downright spiritual concept of why defense matters so much when it comes to winning the game.

Know the Drills

Often in life we are so focused on the glory of scoring and winning that we fail to see the true obstacles in our way that will require us to defend our position, protect our goal or take back what we feel rightfully belongs to us.

Quite the metaphorical type, I really didn't grasp the importance of defense until Fran explained it this way: "Think of your most cherished possession in your home. If it's not a possession, maybe it's a pet, a loved one. Just imagine something you really love and never want to lose. Now imagine someone breaking into your home and stealing or harming that which you most cherish. How does that make you feel? When you step on this basketball court, the basket you defend is your home, and someone attempting to score at your basket is the intruder trying to rob you of your most cherished possession. How much harder can you work, will you work, to do everything in your power to protect and defend your home?"

The light bulb went off for me with a militant glow. I got it. Blow the whistle, Fran; let's do this thing!

From that moment on, I became passionate about defense. I realized I may not always have the greatest shooting game, but I could always give everything I had to defend my goal. I soon learned that the opponents were real, and they seemed to be everywhere. I found this to be most true the more successful I became, or when someone felt threatened or envious, due to his or her own insecurity.

There would be times when I thought I was on top of the world, bothering absolutely no one, and then suddenly I was attacked for trying to maintain my goal of integrity, my goal of dignity, my goal to be a good friend, my goal to be a good

Christian, my goal to just be at peace and mind my own business. The opponents attacked with lies, back stabbing, name calling, two-facedness, false pretenses and petty tactics of envy and resentment. If any part of this sounds familiar to your own situation, then you too should fully understand already why defense is a major part of the game.

You have to be prepared to play unyielding defense because it will always seem when you are trying to reach your goal, the evil opponent, whatever or whomever you conceive it to be, will most certainly take its best shot at trying to discourage you and defeat you. You cannot believe in good without recognizing its direct opposite is evil. In the game of life, these two are constant opponents.

Assuming you are playing for the team of good, you'd be foolish not to prepare yourself to face the team of evil. Keep in mind, however, the team of evil has a way of suiting up sometimes as your closest friend or someone you deeply trust. Sometimes these people consciously choose to play for the evil team. Many more times, they are recruited against their true will. But since they are in their own moments of weakness, they end up on the team they don't really want to play for, because they didn't see any other options. I pity them, but I still condition myself to play against them. It doesn't matter how they got on the team, you just have to know the uniform is different than yours and be determined to not let them get in your house and steal your joy!

Sometimes in life, especially in a work or team environment, you'll find yourself in a bit of a zone defense, where you are relatively relaxed but constantly aware of the opponent's position. You'll allow him to do his thing on the outside, at a distance from you, and you're only prone to aggression if he gets too close.

For instance, for me, such a scenario presented itself when I found myself around peers who were using drugs. Although I made my position clear that I was not interested in participating in the drug scene, I realized there was little I could do or say to keep them from doing so. I determined what they were doing on the outside of my personal circle was beyond my control. But if they tried to enter my personal space and force their will for me to participate, then I would have to more aggressively defend my goal. I wanted to be drug free. I remained in a zone defense on this issue throughout the peer pressures of high school and college, and have continued to do so throughout the rest of my life. It is a particular defensive mentality I hope to successfully pass on to my son and any other youth I might encourage or inspire.

There will be other times where you'll find you have to take on a more aggressive defensive position – in hoops we call it a "man-to-man" defense that puts you directly in the opponent's face and makes it clear to him you have no intention of allowing him to take or destroy what's yours without a fight. Once, a young woman from Harlem expressed to some of my college peers that she hated me because she felt I thought I was better than everyone else. She told them I needed to be taught a lesson. So she threatened to beat me up. She was the rough, thug-type by everyone's standards with a foul mouth and a lot of loud and obnoxious bravado that seemed to frighten everyone to death. The rumor circulated for a week or so, and then one day this crazy woman actually came to the front door of my apartment!

"I just came to let you know I don't like you and I heard you were spreading rumors about me. You don't know a #&*@! thing about me! I'm telling you right here and now, I'm from Harlem, baby, and where I'm from you don't let no lily ass, wannabe white girl dis' you. I better not hear that my name has come out your mouth again or I'm going to kick yo' ass!" she lashed out.

I guess she was fully expecting me to retreat in fear and babble on about my innocence and concern, because she seemed a bit surprised when I stepped up in her face and began the "Soul-sistah-eye-bulging-head-snapping-neck-twisting stare down while informing her, "For the record, if I did say some things about you, they are no worse than the things I've heard you said about me. So we're pretty even on that score. But if you think you're going to walk over here to the front door of my house, flex because you're from Harlem and expect me to be afraid of you, you obviously don't know a #&*@! thing about me either! Ain't no need to wait on the ass-kicking thing, because we can go right now!"

The adrenaline rushing through my soul was playing the theme from Shaft and I felt downright excited that I had cause to let the "Street V" take over the "Sweet V" everyone assumed me to be. The next thing I knew Harlem Queen was mouthing off something about what she better not hear and what I better not say and that I better watch my back, but she was saying it from halfway across the street! All talk and no action. I never had another problem from her again. "Tweet!"

Then there will be times when even more assertiveness is required. You'll devise a full court press in defense of your position or possession. Typically this happens when you have been beaten down or scored on enough times and find yourself in a need to fight back and catch up. Or you may opt to just press all the time because you know the opponent to be one nasty competitor who needs to be challenged before he even gets started with his tactics of offending you.

When you know you are dealing with someone who has constantly lied to you, tried to manipulate you or backstabbed you or others, your best defense is to never give in to allowing yourself to fall for believing in his or her pretentious tactics of goodwill. You simply say, "I will not believe a word this person says. I will proceed with extreme caution whenever he or she is around. I will never let my guard down or else I'm sure I will suffer an agonizing defeat."

Remember that your defense should never be based on fear.

It should be based on wisdom and knowledge that your values, your sanity, your loved ones, your reputation, your possessions, your goals or your life somehow are being threatened or unreasonably compromised. You have a right as well as a responsibility to yourself to play defense, and to play it well.

This would be a good time to add that sometimes, the best defense is just to retreat. That's seldom my recommended option for a real player in the game, but sometimes it's the only realistic option. With that said, never give up fighting for what you know is right, what you believe in, what you stand for, what you value and what you love. You may have to become a better scout of your opponent and the situation you're faced with, and then change your strategy, but you simply cannot give up, unless you decide the goal is no longer worth defending. That is how you know whether to fight or to flee.

Ask yourself, "What is my goal here? Is it worth defending?" Remove the emotion and just deal with the facts. You may have believed a person was honest and true, but when all evidence is pointing toward the fact that he or she is not, you have to trust the facts. Far too many times I've played horrible defense because I didn't want to believe someone close to me would offend me by lying, cheating, stealing, backstabbing or gossiping about me. I'd be totally thrown off my game. I'd spend so much time trying to figure out, "Why could this, why would this, and why did this happen to me?" Meanwhile their goal to manipulate or conquer was succeeding and I was making it easy with questions of offense instead of answers in defense.

When you see a snake, don't waste time wishing it weren't a snake, or that it were a different color snake, or that it were a nicer, more honest or less nasty snake. You immediately say, "Oh shoot, a snake!" and jump into fight or flight defense mode. You recognize the snake, accept the snake for what it is and the harm it does or will do, and that wisdom should be enough to instruct your plan of defense.

You can't allow yourself to be afraid of the snake (yes, this from a woman who jumped out her skin over a roach, let alone a snake!). You just have to be wise about the snake. Just because it seems to smile at you as it lays motionless on the ground doesn't mean it won't slither behind your back and bite you. Adjust your defensive strategy into snake mode and keep on playing the game with your fundamental principles of integrity, dignity and value intact. The last thing you want to do is become a snake yourself. Remember, the evil team is always trying to recruit everyone – even you.

Stand Strong; Defend Yourself

The thing about defense is that it doesn't require as much skill as it requires heart. Yes, you need to be quick and strong, and it definitely helps to be smart. Yet all of these attributes would be moot if you didn't have the drive, determination, courage and commitment to protect yourself, your team or your goal.

In this game, people will talk about you; they will try to hurt you and bring you down. Remember the evil opponent will never want you to win. He is always on the offensive, looking for ways to break you down, including use of trickery like recruiting your friends to play on his team. You have to know when to realize if your friend is now wearing the opponent's jersey.

Play defense first. Ask questions later. The reasons "why" will surface eventually. There's no time for asking "why" when someone is attempting to ruin your reputation, steal your money, disrupt your family, betray your trust, peer pressure you into using drugs, abuse you mentally or physically, or steal your piece of mind. Defend your goal!

In the game of basketball it usually takes an opponent to score a few times and you find yourself at a deficit before you realize you need to step up your defense. There are games, however, when you come out so mentally prepared, so physically conditioned, that you jump all over an opponent with such suffocating defense that they feel defeated before they even get started. Your defense then creates your offensive opportunities, and before you know it the game is a blow out in your favor. You defeat your opponent because you have a plan and the determination to defend your goal that loudly states, "You will not bring trouble here…not in my house…not today… and tomorrow isn't looking good either!"

Be determined to defend your life this way. You will never have to resort to the self pity cry that "life isn't fair." If you're being treated unfairly and you feel like everyone's trying to shoot you down, tighten up the D, baby, and get the ball back! Don't be fooled. Life is awesome! Playing defense is sometimes very tough, but it's also very rewarding.

I wasn't known for being a great basketball defender in my early college playing career. Any of my Syracuse teammates or coaches will tell you that. Nor was I exceptional at it early in my personal or professional life. I've been called a pushover, naïve and too kindhearted more times than I care to admit. But I've grown so much through learning the importance of playing defense.

At the first sign of adversity or of a person who I deduce is likely to bring calamity or misfortune my way, I hear Fran's whistle "Tweet!" I get low in my stance and I get my feet ready to move with my arms spread high and wide. My mind is sharp, and I'm alert and aware that trouble may be coming. If I can get a steal or stop trouble in its tracks, forcing it to turnover and get the ball back in my possession, I double my chances at winning. I know now that in this game of life, just as sure as there will always be a need to play great offense there will also always be a time and a need to play great defense. They are both equally important. For which is truly more valuable: the goal you seek to conquer, or the one you must defend?

When you come to play the game understanding they are both equally important, that's when you win games. Let me go on record to add…that's how you win championships!

POST-GAME...
Play Through The Foul!

December 28, 2008

Another year has just about come to an end. I sit on the balcony of the Wyndham Oceanwalk Resort in Daytona Beach, Florida. It's 6:56 a.m. God is busy at work painting yet another fabulous sunrise out on the horizon. The ocean waves and little white seagulls sing in discordant unison a melody only they seem to know, but it is so very soothing and pleasing to my ears. I am amazed at how what was a pitch black night only an hour ago when I stepped out onto my balcony is now the most spectacular canvas of gold, orange, pink, purple and blue light, softly decorated with little fluffy gray clouds.

As I sip my freshly brewed hazelnut coffee, I realize God paints a breathtaking picture this way every morning over the various shores of our universe. The color schemes may vary, but the theme is always the same: the light always follows the darkness; the dawn always follows the dusk; and the night always becomes the day. Just as He created Heaven and Earth in the beginning, He recreates this thematic backdrop and flow-of-life reminder for us daily.

I take another sip of coffee as the smell of hope seems to fill the beach air. My mind drifts to the thoughts of Barack Obama, the son of an African man and a white mother, who was elected President of the United States only a month and change ago. His election came crashing through the stigma and cynicism of prejudice, oppression and the injustices that had far too long held this country back because of its shameful, racially intolerant and hateful history.

President-elect Obama will inherit nagging questions over the pain of war abroad in Iraq and the biggest recession since the Great Depression. Critics deem his challenges insurmountable in the face of a country demanding change and surviving on hope, the two thematic promises his Democratic party rode to victory. I wonder how on earth this man will be able to deliver on his promises.

But then I am reminded that Barack Obama is a "baller" with a smooth lefty jump shot. His love of the game of hoops has been well documented throughout his campaign and election. Suddenly I chuckle as I say to myself, "Barack's got game. I bet he knows all about playing through the foul."

I believe this country, even with all of its haters who will find a way to kick, scratch, claw, elbow and hack this poor man to near death, will still be okay, and our country will soon thrive. Out loud now I'm muttering, "'Change We Can Believe In' was your campaign slogan, but I'm thinking you might need 'Play Through the Foul' as your mantra in office, Mr. President! I've trademarked it, but it's yours to use if you want it!"

This morning, I'm realizing the awesome power of change and hope as I look back over the past decade of my life and feel my spirit now trying to paint its own sunrise. Maybe it's the coffee, but suddenly I can't stop thinking about all the things I've come through to arrive at this moment. Perhaps it's the ambiance causing the rapid flow of memories. After all, this is the very same beach I was married on eleven years ago. This is the same beach I came to when after my divorce, and in need of a girlfriend getaway, my two closest friends and I decided we should go on a vacation together. They picked a date I was unavailable to go, citing "a deal they just couldn't pass up" as justification. Despite my hurt and pleading, they chose to go on a cruise without me, waking me up to the harsh reality that I was not quite as important in their world as I had held them in mine.

I headed to the beach every time I felt things were going sour with my career. I headed to the beach every time I was heartbroken. I spent a night crying on the beach when my mother died. I headed to the beach to pray when I needed forgiveness for the fouls I too had committed. When I was broke and broken, betrayed and dismayed, dejected and rejected, juggling and struggling, I came to the beach.

Today, however, I sit at the beach feeling no pain because I'm focused on finishing a book about how I played through the fouls. I'm witnessing how commitment, persistence and faith rhythmically need to move together as we weave through the dance and the game of life. I'm filled with the significance of the sunrise. Were it not for the darkness, we'd never recognize morning's true beauty. The sunrise is change. It is hope. It is the absolute most beautiful reminder of why we play through the fouls. I came here to the beach so that my final chapter would be inspired to offer you the greatest thoughts of change and of hope in your life in a way a basketball lover could only present it.

An Eight-Year Journey

Eight years ago I set out to become a writer. Eight years! You'd think in that time I would have written eight books and eighty thousand pages! However, in those eight years, this book was writing me. It was teaching me very valuable lessons about life. How on earth could I truly write about fouls that I never really endured? What would make me a convincing "life coach" if I'd never really played the game? I had no idea what was happening as I was going through some of life's fouls, but today upon completion of this final chapter, I get it. I get all of it. These eight chapters represent those eight years of growth.

The writing of this book has endured five title and theme changes; a heart breaking divorce; seven moves through four states; unemployment; a half dozen job or career changes; liars, cheaters, schemers and opportunists often disguised as friends; the painfully scarred lives of young women who have come under my trust, tutelage, mentoring or care; friends who have needed a place to stay as they got their own lives back on track; the death of my mother and closest aunt; hernia surgery followed by hemorrhoid surgery ten months later; a 9-1-1 call and the subsequent hospitalization of my then seven-year-old son who fought for his life in the Asthma Ward of Children's Hospital with a collapsed left lung; the burglary of my home earlier this year where my then half-finished manuscript was totally lost because my laptop and flash drives were stolen; and finally, 99 unsuccessful diets and weight-loss regimens.

Every one of these distractions and disappointments has had their place in the game. They are called life fouls. I don't profess that my fouls are any harder felt than the next person's. I just know they exist and they hurt. They hurt most when they are inflicted intentionally or caused by someone we love or whom we want to love us. But I also know that we get through them because, well...because we have to. It's the only way to play the game. The victories are far sweeter than the defeats. That's what makes the game worth playing.

As I replay as many fouls as my mind can muster in one early morning, hazelnut coffee-enhanced sitting, I relate them all somehow to the writing of this book you are holding today. I'm in awe of the now evident fact that the writing of this book was not hindered or distracted by the fouls; it was made possible because of them!

I had a dream to become a writer eight years ago. That dream was prophetically endorsed and encouraged by my mother two weeks prior to her death when she said that she wished I would give up coaching basketball and finish writing that book I had started years ago, get on the speaker's circuit and teach people. She said I was talented at so many things but I could never quite finish anything because I wasn't applying myself to my true purpose. My giving back was in telling my stories and inspiring people to find their own passions and purposes and help them get over their own problems and pains.

I never thought that was actually my gift. I guess at times I was far too consumed in my own bitterness, shortcomings and frustrations to consider how far I had actually come to get through them all, and how my faith sustained me to be stronger because of them.

Life is full of adversity. I've learned that adversity is not only inevitable, but absolutely necessary, for how else may we truly measure how much we've grown? So before you think of quitting because life is too tough, the game is just too unfair, please consider this: **"The closer you are to the goal, the harder the foul ™."** You may be closer to scoring and winning than you realize.

Sure you can stand around on the perimeter tossing up wild shots and praying they go in. A few of them actually will. But when you want to be sure you are taking the highest percentage, highest quality shot available to you, you have to be prepared to do what it takes to grind it out, drive into that key and power that ball up in the face of adversity. In this game, you have to **KNOW IT'S A CONTACT SPORT**, so you have to: **GET IN SHAPE AND STAY IN SHAPE; BE COACHABLE; HANDLE THE BALL; MAKE THE ASSIST; REBOUND RELENTLESSLY; PASSIONATELY PLAY YOUR POSITION; and DEFEND YOUR GOAL**.

Game On!

When it's all said and done, be sure to make time to sit back and appreciate the applause. There may be fans outwardly cheering for you, as I can be especially thankful for my son

Andrew, my best friend Jan, and for the great advice from my friend Karen, an awesome writer, whose applause has been particularly the loudest during the writing of this book. There are so many others whose cheers throughout life we could never have done without, particularly for me, the cheers of my mother and my father. Still it is the silent sunrise of applause from within that resound the loudest as you realize playing through the fouls has brought you to several, undeniably important victories. Ultimately you will have learned acceptance that the fouls in the game are inevitable, and if you're going to play then you're going to get fouled.

You gain strength in playing through those fouls. You'll learn forgiveness as you realize those who have fouled you aren't perfect or necessarily malicious…and by the way, neither are you. You'll experience joy because there are so many times when you will make a beautiful assist, you will grab an all important rebound, and you will score – sometimes many baskets, and sometimes only a few – but the fact remains you *will* score.

Finally, you will gain wisdom that comes from just playing and even coaching the game as you mature through and into your real purpose and position on the team. Then you will be at peace, for the Ultimate Coach will be pleased, and you will know it. It will be a peace that settles in your soul much like mine did this morning at sunrise, where off in the distance I could see and feel the tears of joy resounding from my mother's spirit that this book is now complete. I'm trusting that she was right, that I have a gift, and that this gift now serves to be the assist I need to inspire you to stop worrying so much about the fouls and just get out there play your best game ever.

The sun is high in the sky now in pursuit of a predicted, toasty 79 degrees in December on this beach. Kids are laughing and splashing in the waves, adults are tanning poolside, Frisbees and music rock the sandy shores. It's a picture perfect day. I'm so thankful God lets me get in the game and play again today. It's been a hectic yet amazing year. Actually, it's been a hectic and amazing life. One day I hope to share even more of it with you.

For now, I thank you for reading this book. I pray it has touched you, encouraged you and coached you to want to be the absolutely best player you can be. If it has, then I've not only played through the foul, but I just hit my free throw! An uncontrollable tear of joy flows out of my soul down my cheek. I get this game. I love this game. I hope you do too!

Best "Swishes!"

ABOUT VERA JONES

Audiences large and small across the country have been captivated and motivated by this "naturally gifted" public speaker, award-winning television and radio broadcaster, and Hall of Fame athlete. Vera is most notably known for her extensive background in broadcasting, serving as a National Collegiate Athletic Association and WNBA Basketball Color Analyst and Reporter. She has been an on-air personality at several radio stations from New York to Florida, earning the South Carolina Broadcaster's Association "Personality of the Year" award in 1994. Over recent years, she has groomed her training, mentoring and leadership skills in the arena of collegiate coaching. She currently spends the NCAA Women's Basketball season broadcasting for the Big Ten Network.

A 2002 inductee into the Syracuse University Orange Plus Hall of Fame, Vera was also recognized as the 1988 Big East Women's Basketball conference Scholar-Athlete of the Year. She earned both her Bachelor's and Master's degrees from Syracuse University's renowned Newhouse School of Public Communications. In addition to 20 years of fulfillment as a broadcasting and media professional, her diverse background has invited her to wear many other exciting hats: coach, teacher, academic advisor, trainer, sales and promotions manager, program director, writer, real estate agent, actress, and stand-up comedienne. As a communicator, she's truly been there, done that! Vera's "first big speech" came when she was asked to deliver the commencement address in front of an audience of over 2,000 at her high school graduation. Over two decades and hundreds of public speeches later, her "gift of gab" is still in demand.

Vera's penchant for empowering and entertaining has been cultivated by employment and training opportunities by prominent corporate, media and academic industry leaders. They include Procter & Gamble, Pulte Homes, ESPN, Fox Sports, Madison Square Garden, NBA/WNBA, NCAA, Syracuse University, Indiana University, the University of Dayton, and the Paul Robeson Performing Arts Company. Using a unique and interactive blend of wit and wisdom, Vera has parlayed her wealth of personal and professional experiences, into a motivational public speaking and communications training career. Thus, not only are people gratifyingly discovering why Vera's VoiceWorks, but how confidently and effectively theirs can work too!

NOTES

NOTES